SYRIA

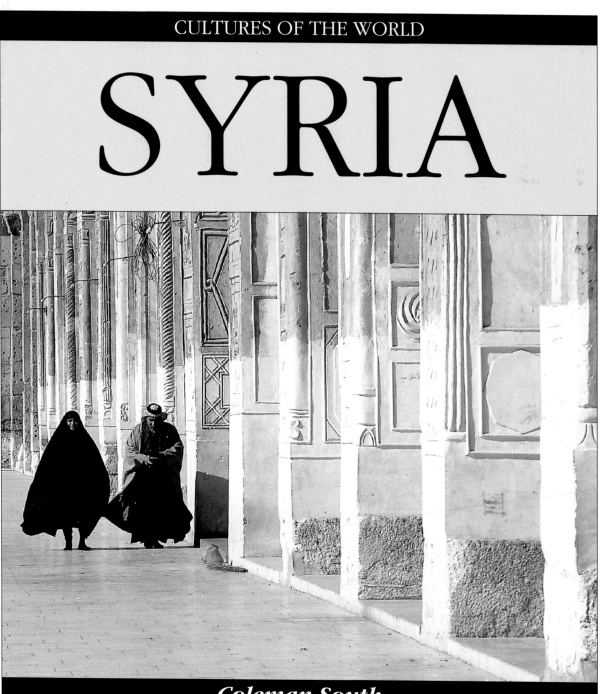

Coleman South

MARSHALL CAVENDISH
New York • London • Sydney

Reference edition published 1995 by
Marshall Cavendish Corporation
2415 Jerusalem Avenue
P.O. Box 587
North Bellmore
New York 11710

Originated and designed by
Times Books International, an imprint of
Times Editions Pte Ltd

Printed in Singapore

Library of Congress Cataloging-in-Publication Data:
South, Coleman.
      Syria / Coleman South.
         p. cm.—(Cultures Of The World)
      Includes bibliographical references (p.) and index.
      ISBN 0-7614-0172-5 (Syria)
      ISBN 0-7614-0167-9 (Set)
      1. Syria—Juvenile literature. [1. Syria] I. Title.
II. Series.
DS93.S66 1995
956.91—dc20   94–43359
                              CIP
                                AC

Cultures of the World

Editorial Director	Shirley Hew
Managing Editor	Shova Loh
Editors	Elizabeth Berg
	Dinah Lee
	Azra Moiz
	Sue Sismondo
Picture Editor	Susan Jane Manuel
Production	Anthoney Chua
Design	Tuck Loong
	Felicia Wong
	Loo Chuan Ming
	Wendy Koh
Illustrators	Chow Kok Keong
	Anuar bin Abdul Rahim
MCC Editorial Director	Evelyn M. Fazio

INTRODUCTION

SOME OF THE WORLD'S EARLIEST civilizations thrived in what is now Syria. The first known alphabet was discovered in Ugarit on the north Syrian coast. The country has remains from the Sumerians, Babylonians, Egyptians, Hittites, Canaanites (Phoenicians), Assyrians, Persians, Greeks, Romans, Arabs, Ottomans, and French. There are about 200 historical and archeological sites and most likely others that have yet to be discovered.

All of the settlers and conquerors have left their mark in some way, and the Syrian people are proud of their diverse cultural heritage and their ancestral mix, even though they consider themselves to be Arabs. They are a funloving people who are exceptionally hospitable to visitors.

Islam influences virtually every aspect of life. The amplified call to prayer, five times daily from thousands of mosque minarets, adds a timeless rhythm to daily life.

CONTENTS

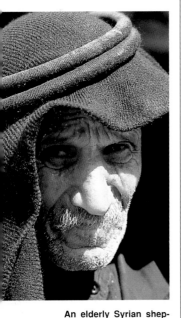

An elderly Syrian shepherd.

CONTENTS

A geometric animal motif typical of Islamic art.

5

GEOGRAPHY

MODERN SYRIA was once part of a larger area that included what are now the countries of Syria, Jordan, Lebanon, and Israel. This land has been called the Levant, Greater Syria, and in Arabic, *Bilad al Sham* ("bi-LAD uh-SHAM"). It is still often referred to as the Levant.

Geography, vegetation, and weather in Syria are varied, ranging from mountains to steppes, from lush vegetation to barren land, and from moderate to extreme temperatures. Two-thirds of Syria is desert.

LOCATION AND SIZE

Syria borders Jordan on the south, Lebanon on the west, Israel on the southwest, the Mediterranean Sea on the northwest, Turkey on the north, and Iraq on the east and southeast. It has about 90 miles (145 km) of Mediterranean coastline.

The country is shaped somewhat like a triangle with irregular sides. You can drive from any border to any other in less than one day. Although it covers only about 71,500 square miles (185,180 sq km), just slightly more than North Dakota, Syria's strategic location has increased its historical importance to both Middle Eastern and Western civilizations far out of proportion to its size. It is often called "the crossroads of civilizations."

Syria has one Mediterranean island, called Arwad, just off the coast at Tartus. The island was an independent kingdom called Aradus in the days of the Phoenicians and contains many historical structures as well as a marina. Its inhabitants depend on fishing for their livelihoods.

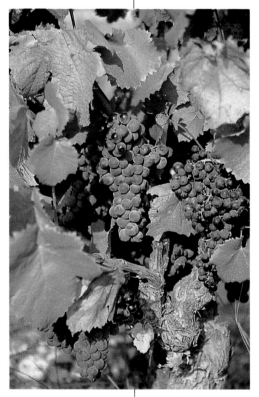

Opposite: **Poppies cover a field in western Syria.**

Above: **Grapes grow in abundance along the coast and in the coastal mountains.**

7

GEOGRAPHIC REGIONS AND CLIMATE

The western band of the country, where most of the people live, is less than 60 miles (100 km) wide and has a Mediterranean climate. The coastal plain is one of the most fertile on the Mediterranean. Temperatures range between 70-90° F (21–32° C) in summer and 50-70° F (10–21° C) in winter. It is humid at the coast, with annual rainfall averaging 38 inches (96 cm).

Next is a range of limestone mountains called the Jabal al-Nusayriya, which are cool in summer, cold and often snow-covered in the winter. Between this range and the next one is a drier but still fertile valley called the Gharb Depression, which was filled with marshes in ancient times.

Next comes a range of dry mountains. The climate on and near this eastern range is similar, but with warmer summer temperatures and colder winter temperatures than on the coast. The narrow strip of land along the eastern slopes of the coastal mountains is where the largest cities are, and the climate varies quite a bit from south to north. For example, the average rainfall in Aleppo, in the north, is about 18.5 inches (47 cm) per year, but it is only nine inches (22.8 cm) in Damascus, farther south. But the rainfall again increases south of Damascus. The temperatures along this strip range from over 100° F (37° C) in summer to below freezing in winter.

The reason for the drier area around Damascus is the Anti-Lebanon Mountains. The western spine of this range is in Lebanon and is higher than the coastal mountains of Syria. The eastern spine is higher yet and turns northeastward at Damascus. They end in the geographic center of Syria, east of Palmyra ("pal-MEER-a"), and block most rainfall.

The area east of the populated strip, with the exception of some mountainous land along the Turkish border and the irrigated land along the three main rivers, is high steppe and rocky, gravel desert. The Syrian Desert, as it is named, also covers a large part of eastern Jordan, western Iraq, and northern Saudi Arabia.

The desert on the south bank of the Euphrates has traditionally supported Bedouin herds.

The desert in south-central Syria is an ancient volcanic area covered by rough lava flows and dotted with cinder cones. Some of this land has been painstakingly cleared of lava rock so it can be used for agriculture.

9

The Euphrates River supported many early civilizations.

RIVERS

There are several large rivers. The Euphrates enters from Turkey in the northwest, travels east for a ways, then south again, exiting into Iraq in the southeast. It has two tributaries. The Al Balikh River also starts in Turkey, enters Syria in the north, and flows into the Euphrates in north central Syria. The Al Khabur begins in the northeast and flows into the Euphrates at Deirez-Zor, about 100 miles (160 km) from the Iraqi border.

The Barada is a small river that creates the Al-Ghuta Oasis, where the capital stands. The Barada begins in several mountain springs near Damascus and flows northeastward. Although it nearly dries up in the dry season, it has allowed people to live in Damascus for thousands of years.

The Orontes has its sources near Homs and flows northward through the Gharb Depression into Turkey, then empties into the Mediterranean. Dams at Homs and Hama ("ha-MA") on the Orontes have made western Syria agriculturally productive and provided local industry with hydropower.

LIQUID LIFE, LIQUID POWER

The Euphrates River, at 2,100 miles (3,360 km) long, is the largest river in western Asia. It begins on the Armenian Plateau in eastern Turkey and joins the Tigris River at Basra in southern Iraq, where the two rivers create vast marshlands. Turkey has 40% of the river's length inside its borders, Syria only 15%, but this small portion has supported civilization in eastern and northern Syria for thousands of years. Although the river is quite wide (in some places nearly a mile), it is mostly shallow with constantly shifting sandbars, and ships cannot navigate it.

The primary use of the river today is for irrigation, although it also provides some fish. Its second most important use is for the generation of electrical power. Construction of the Tabaqah Dam near Aleppo was begun in 1968 after extensive archeological exploration of the upstream portion that would be flooded by the lake. This is Syria's major source of electricity and its only dam on the Euphrates. The dam creates the largest lake in Syria, Lake Al Asad, which is about 50 miles long and an average of five miles wide. It holds about 15,600,000 cubic yards (12 million cu m) of water.

There are bound to be conflicts among countries that share such a major river in an arid region, and Syria is upset with Turkey because it has built several dams on the Euphrates, blocking the flow to Syria and reducing the amount of electrical power it can produce. This reduced flow is part of the reason for Syria's regular power outages. Food is more important than electricity, so the water flow that supports agriculture below Al Tabaqah must be maintained, even if it means less electricity.

ISLANDS IN THE DESERT

One of the things that has made life possible in this part of the world is oases. These are lowland places where natural springs surface and allow plants to grow. The most common plants are date palms, but some oases grow bananas and olives as well. Many of the palm trees are centuries old.

There are always small settlements around the water sources, some of them thousands of years old. In the past, these settlements served as caravansaries—resting places for camel caravans.

The spring water is channeled by small canals through plots of land that are often surrounded by ancient adobe walls 6-8 feet (2–2.5 m) high. These canals may have been the world's first irrigation systems.

There are a few oases, the biggest and best known one at Tadmor, near the ruins of Palmyra. This oasis was the source of life for the Roman city.

Lush foliage at the oasis at Palmyra.

LAKES

Syria has only two natural lakes. The others were created by dams built for irrigation and electrical power. The biggest of the natural lakes is Arram, which fills the crater of an extinct volcano in the Golan Heights. The other natural lake is Mzerib, northeast of Daraa, which is on the border with Jordan.

The largest artificial lake is Lake Al Asad, created by the Tabaqah Dam. The second largest lake is Qattina, southwest of Homs. This is the main source of the Orontes River, and although it used to be rich with fish, it is now badly contaminated. Another lake, about one-third the size of Qattina, is Al Rastan, formed by a dam on the Orontes River about 12 miles (20 km) north of Homs. About 9 miles (15 km) north of Hama is Lake Karma, another source of water for the Orontes. Lake Baloran is in the mountains northeast of Latakia, created by a dam on the river of the same name. And finally, Lake Karn is a tiny lake in the mountains west of Damascus, formed by a dam on the Barada River.

CITIES

About half of Syria's population live in cities. Syria's cities have a few modern elements, but they look ancient. Some have narrow, winding streets, and many buildings have not changed in hundreds of years.

Damascus is one of the oldest continuously inhabited cities in the world. Ancient Damascus lies on the southern bank of the Barada River. One of its most famous landmarks is the Omayyad Mosque, which was constructed in A.D. 705. Modern Damascus extends north of the Barada. It has wide avenues, large apartment buildings, and tall office complexes. The University of Damascus sits on the outskirts.

Aleppo is also an ancient city, with the earliest settlements dating from about 7,000 years ago. A large 12th-century Arab fort dominates the older part of the city. Modern Aleppo is a commercial and industrial center.

Homs, a heavy industry center, and Latakia, the country's main port on the Mediterranean, were both established by the Greeks around 300 B.C.

Damascus is the commercial capital of Syria.

Deir-ez-Zor is the center of oil exploration. It is located on the Euphrates River in the southeast, about 60 miles (100 km) from Iraq.

Lizards are common in the desert. Here an *Agama Ruderata* basks in the sun in the Syrian Desert.

FLORA AND FAUNA

Along the coast and in the coastal mountains, pine, olive, and fruit trees and grapevines are abundant. The cities east of the coastal range have green belts around them where most of their fruits and vegetables have traditionally been grown. This is changing, though, with population growth, and the bigger cities now bring most of their produce from rural areas farther away. In and around Damascus, Homs, Hama, and Aleppo, there are olive, eucalyptus, pine, locust, maple, fig, palm, and citrus trees and also many grapevines. Poplars and cottonwoods grow along the rivers on the eastern side of the coastal mountains, and of course, palm trees grow in desert oases and on the edges of the desert. In the cities, jasmine, bougainvillea, orange blossoms, and other flowers provide splashes of color and sweet scents during spring and summer.

No official statistics exist about what animals still roam the deserts and mountains and which ones are endangered or extinct. However, less than a century ago, gazelles, lions, eagles, buzzards, jackals, red foxes, desert hares, and wolves were common. Arab princes used to fight the lions as part of their coming-into-manhood ritual. They also staged large hunting expeditions for desert creatures. Scorpions, lizards, and snakes are common in the deserts.

Sadly, it seems that most larger wildlife in Syria is already gone or on the way to disappearing. The little that remains—gazelles and foxes, for example—are still hunted for sport.

There are probably several reasons for the disappearance of the ancient wildlife. One is human population growth and its encroachment in all fertile areas of the country. Another is the use of DDT and other poisons that are banned in most Western countries. Yet another is the wild dogs in the desert, the offspring of the wolf-like dogs kept by Bedouins to protect their sheep. These fierce animals often run in packs and will even attack people. Underlying all these reasons is the fact that people in this part of the world have little appreciation for wildlife.

Another reason may be climate change. Over the past few centuries a lot of land that used to be fertile has become desert. In the central desert, for example, there are ruins of Arab palaces that were used in part as hunting lodges. To build and use such permanent structures required regular supplies of food, water, and fuel, none of which is there now.

The Syrian desert is different from most deserts in the United States, which support a profusion of life. There is little vegetation other than sparse clumps of short grass in the late winter and early spring and the greenery in a few oases. The grass of the desert and steppes, however, supports Bedouin ("BED-win") sheep and goats as it has for millennia.

Gagea reticulata blooms in a Syrian desert.

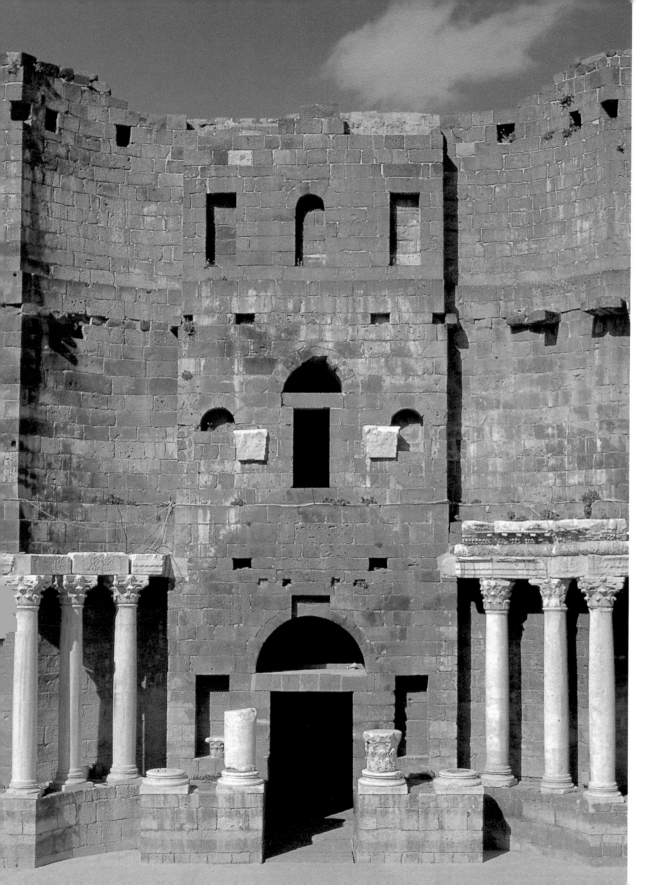

HISTORY

SYRIA HAS A RICH and culturally diverse history. The coast and the Euphrates River area have remnants of empires and diverse civilizations from as far back as 7,000 years. There are structures that are still used that were built by the Romans, the early Arabs, the Ottomans, and the French.

ANCIENT HISTORY

The earliest prehistoric remains of people found in Syria are from the Middle Paleolithic period. The fertility goddesses and flint and obsidian tools of early peoples have been found in Ugarit, on the Syrian coast.

A thousand years later, settlers began using primitive soft pottery. Then, 4,000 to 5,000 years ago, ceramics in elegant shapes, painted with geometric designs, began to appear. The technology of the pottery slowly improved, and during the first millennium B.C. copper work appeared.

Until around the eighth century B.C., Syria had two mostly separate histories: eastern and western. West of the coastal mountains, the Phoenicians and Aramaeans flourished; in the eastern part of what is now Syria, the Sumerians and the Babylonians built their civilizations.

Opposite: **The Roman theater at Busra. The Romans left many impressive ruins that are still visible today.**

Left: **An archeological dig in the Euphrates area of northern Syria. Pottery from early settlers has been found all across northern Syria.**

Several tablets, including a letter from the Hittite king, had not yet been baked when the destruction of Ugarit began. Was it a warning that came too late to be heeded? And who destroyed the city? We may never know the answers.

WESTERN HISTORY

Around 2000 B.C. the Canaanites moved onto the coastal plain and the seaward side of the coastal mountains in what is now Israel, Lebanon, and Syria. These people were called Phoenicians by the Greeks. This name referred to all the peoples of the area, although none of them called themselves by that name.

The Phoenicians were the first great seafarers, establishing colonies and trading with people all around the Aegean Sea. It was during their time that the already ancient settlement at Ugarit was given its name. They developed and improved iron tools, and had the first royalty that wore purple robes. The purple dye came from a mollusk unique to the Mediterranean shores of Syria. The first known kings were Niqmadou and Yaqaroum. During the 15th century B.C., the Egyptians invaded and conquered parts of Syria but left the Canaanite kingdom intact; the two groups were friendly.

The earliest known alphabetic writing dates from the reign of Niqmadou II (about 1360-1330 B.C.). The writing, in alphabetic cuneiform on tablets, tells much about the customs and institutions of the coastal people. The tablets show that the Canaanite kingdom included a large part of what is now northwestern Syria. They speak of extensive diplomatic activity to safeguard the kingdom from the advance of both the Egyptians on the south and the Hittites on the north.

Thereafter trade, war, and political intrigue became increasingly common among the peoples at this end of the Mediterranean, and Ugarit was finally destroyed around the end of the 13th century B.C. The city never rose again, but during the fifth and fourth centuries B.C., Greek fishers built some dwellings there, atop a hill that buried thousands of years of history, and named the place Leukos Limen.

LANGUAGE AT UGARIT

The development of written language may be the most significant aspect of Syrian history. There were two original types of writing: the hieroglyphic style of Egypt and the alphabetic cuneiform style discovered at Ugarit and in ancient Sumer. Cuneiform was the simplest, consisting of only 30 shapes, one for each letter. The Phoenician alphabet was later used as the basis for Greek, which in turn was the basis for most Western alphabets. Arabic also has its roots in Ugaritic.

The language represented by cuneiform characters—called Ugaritic—was one of several languages used in Ugarit. It was spoken by most of the city's population and was used in poems and myths. Babylonian, the international language of the time, was used in diplomatic correspondence and judicial documents. Most of the texts found are in these two languages—Ugaritic and Babylonian—but others have been found in Hurrian (a non-Semitic language of eastern Asia Minor), Cypro-Minoan, Hittite and Sumerian cuneiform, and Egyptian and Hittite hieroglyphics.

ARAMAEANS Around the end of the 13th century B.C., about the same time as the Israelites migrated into Phoenicia, another Semitic people, known as the Aramaeans, settled east of the coastal mountains. Their kingdom became known as Aram and eventually covered a large part of what is now Syria.

From their capital in Damascus, the Aramaeans developed extensive overland trade with southern Arabia and Persia. They converted the Phoenician alphabet for use with their own language, Aramaic, which became the official language of Syria.

Around 1030 B.C., the Aramaean tribes joined together to attack the Israelites under the leadership of David but were defeated in three campaigns. The Aramaeans and the Israelites continued to struggle for domination of the area until the eighth century B.C.

Aram prospered for hundreds of years before being destroyed by the Assyrians in 732 B.C.

Aramaic, which is the language Christ spoke, is still spoken today in and around Maalula ("ma-a-LOO-la"), a village north of Damascus, and is used in the liturgy of the Syrian Orthodox Church.

A Hittite statue from Tal Halaf in Aleppo dates from the ninth century B.C.

EASTERN HISTORY

Aroung 3000 B.C., the ancient Sumerians (of what is now southern Iraq) spread northeastward into what is now eastern Syria and northern Iraq, eventually occupying most of the land between and around the Euphrates and Tigris Rivers. The area is often referred to as Mesopotamia, the Fertile Crescent, and Babylonia. The people became known as Babylonians. Mari, an archeological site on the Euphrates River near the Iraqi border, has turned up evidence of settlers as far back as the second century B.C. (In 1933, the remains of a 300-room palace were uncovered here—one of the biggest palaces ever discovered!)

At the same time the Babylonians were developing and expanding, the civilization of the Assyrians was developing on the northern Tigris River. The Assyrians, from which Syria got its name, were as well known for their military conquests and brutality as the Babylonians were for their accomplishments in science, the arts, and religion.

In 2300 B.C., a group of Semitic people under a leader known as Sargon conquered Babylonia and established the kingdom of Akkad. Not long after, this kingdom fell to Guti tribes from the Zagros mountains between modern Turkey and Iran. In the 19th century B.C., Amorites, descendants of the Canaanites, conquered the region. The Assyrians took over all of Babylonia in the 14th century B.C. A hundred years later, they had occupied most of Syria and Phoenicia. But in the 10th century the Aramaeans drove them back.

EMPIRES

In the eighth century B.C., the Assyrians returned and conquered all of Syria, ending the separate historical development. This empire did not last long, though: in the seventh century B.C., the land was conquered by the Babylonians under Nebuchadnezzar. A hundred years later, Syria became part of the Persian Empire. Then, in 333 B.C., Alexander the Great conquered it, and it remained a Greek outpost until the Romans under Pompey added Syria to the Roman Empire in 64 B.C. .

The period of Roman rule was prosperous and much building was accomplished. The Romans have left the largest number of remains in Syria: cities, amphitheaters, temples, and forts from Turkey to Jordan and the Mediterranean coast to the Euphrates River. Damascus became famous for its architecture and its schools of law and medicine. Palmyra, a trading center for caravans, reached its height in the third century A.D.

In A.D. 395 the Roman Empire split into east and west. Syria became part of the eastern, or Byzantine, empire. The Byzantine rulers, who were Christian, tried to convert the Syrians but were successful only in the north.

There were three Roman emperors who came from Syria. One was Philip, who ruled the empire from A.D. 244 to 249. His birthplace of Shahba has ruins of a Roman theater, Roman baths, and a museum of well-preserved mosaic floors. The other two emperors came from Homs (called Emesa at that time), 100 miles north of Damascus: Alexander (Lucius) Severus (193-211), and Elagabalus (218-222).

Ruins of an aqueduct at Palmyra. The Romans destroyed Palmyra in 272.

Zenobia in Chains, an 1859 sculpture by Harriet Hosmer.

QUEEN ZENOBIA

Smack in the middle of Syria, about 150 miles from the nearest city, stand the remains of Palmyra, an extensive and beautiful Roman city that was built in the 3rd century A.D.. In A.D. 260, a man named Odenathus was given the title "king of Palmyra" by the Roman Emperor. His wife's name was Zenobia ("zih-NO-bee-ah"), and little is known about her before she married him, except that she was one of the best-educated women of her time and was an expert linguist. There are rumors that she was half Arab and half Greek—but this has not been confirmed.

Odenathus died in 267, and it is suspected that Zenobia had a hand in his death. Zenobia proclaimed herself queen, although she was officially acting as regent for her baby son. For a while, she appeared to defend Roman interests in the area, but starting in 268 she embarked on a conquest for herself. Her armies took over all of Syria, ventured into Egypt in 269, and by 270 had conquered all of Asia Minor, building fortifications at strategic points to defend her realm. In 270, Aurelian was elected the new Roman emperor, and at about the same time, Zenobia proclaimed her still-infant son, Septimius Vaballathus Athenodorus, emperor.

Aurelian became alarmed at the ambitions of Zenobia and sent a trusted general to recapture Egypt. He himself went after the queen of the desert, defeating her army in Antioch (now Antakya, Turkey) and at Emesa (now Homs, Syria) in 271. He then reached Palmyra, which Zenobia defended for some time; but the city surrendered and was razed by his troops in 273.

The story then goes that Zenobia and her son were captured by Roman soldiers as they fled Palmyra, and when the soldiers wanted to kill her, she saved her life by blaming her ministers and allowing them to be executed in her place, including one who had been her linguistic tutor. Whatever happened, Aurelian marched triumphantly back to Rome in the year 274 with the rebel queen in tow on a golden chain, bound with golden shackles, and covered with expensive jewelry. Some say she married a Roman senator. She did live out the remainder of her life in a villa at Tibur (now Tivoli). Aurelian also pardoned her son and married her daughters into influential Roman families.

Queen Zenobia is an important figure for many Syrian women. When the men here say a woman should only do certain kinds of work, that she cannot lead a country or an army, many women counter with, "What about our Queen Zenobia?" Even though her reign was short, she challenged the world's largest empire and held off its armies for several years. Perhaps equally important, she was successful in defeat, earning the respect of the very people she had tried to outdo.

A sculpture from Palmyra at the time of Zenobia.

The Omayyad Mosque is one of the oldest in the world and is still used every day.

THE OMAYYADS

Although all of the civilizations and empires left their mark on Syria in some way, it was the zeal of Islam that changed it permanently and forms the basis of modern Syrian society.

After the Prophet Mohammed's death, his followers were divided over who should lead them. The Shi'as ("SHE-ahs") argued that it must be a member of the Prophet's family and chose Ali, the Prophet's son-in-law. The majority of followers, the Sunnis ("SOON-neez"), wanted to elect caliphs to rule in his place. Immediate animosity developed between the two groups and continues today.

In addition to this split, there were conflicts between clans struggling for political and religious power. The Omayyads ("oh-MY-yads") were initially the strongest of these clans. Led by Khalid ibn al-Walid, they conquered Damascus in 636, and most of the population adopted Islam.

The Omayyads ruled most of the Arab empire from Busra, in southern Syria, from the mid-seventh to the mid-eighth centuries. They continued in their drive to spread Islam by the sword and eventually extended the Arab empire to include the entire Arabian Peninsula, northern Africa as far as the Atlantic Ocean, and southern Europe—an area about the same size as the former Roman Empire.

After the Omayyads took over in the seventh century A.D., Arabic spread as the common language of the land. Although Christianity had strongholds in the mountains of western Syria, the only religion that was able to take hold uniformly was Islam, and it has had an overriding influence on the country's development and direction. Adherents of other religions were, however, allowed to continue to practice their religion.

The Omayyads built roads, founded hospitals, and encouraged education. Scholars from other lands studied in Damascus, developing new medical practices and philosophical ideas. The Omayyad Empire is considered to be a high point of Islamic civilization.

Under the Omayyads, however, political administration, education, intellectual pursuits, and other aspects of city life were more highly valued than rural life. This caused conflict between the predominantly rural inhabitants of the Middle East and the urban dwellers. That conflict, combined with the strife between Sunni and Shi'a groups and among clans, finally overpowered the Omayyads around the middle of the eighth century. The Babylonians, who were Shi'as, conquered the area but neglected the coastal areas, which fell under the control of Egypt.

The first Arabs left a landmark in the lovely Omayyad Mosque in Damascus. This was built in the seventh century over the ruins of the Cathedral of St. John, which in turn was built over a Roman temple. It contains a sepulcher that Muslims believe holds the head of John the Baptist.

The siege of Damascus during the Second Crusade is illustrated in the late 15th-century French manuscript, *Conqueror of Jerusalem.*

THE CRUSADERS

During the 10th and 11th centuries, Greater Syria developed many local principalities and emirates, and this political fragmentation allowed invading French Crusaders to take over much of northern and western Syria. The Crusaders came in waves, building mighty hilltop fortresses that still stand. A big part of the battle between the Crusaders and the Muslims and Jews was for Jerusalem, which was a holy city to all of them.

Despite their success on the coastal plains and in the coastal mountains, however, the Crusaders never had much impact in central and eastern Syria, and the cities of Damascus, Homs, and Hama were never taken.

In 1169 the Syrian sultan Nureddin sent his general Salah al-Din (commonly called Saladin, "sa-LAD-din") to the Egyptian royal court. Saladin took control of Egypt in 1171 and after Nureddin's death became sultan of both Egypt and Syria. He attacked the Crusaders and pushed the European armies out of Jerusalem in 1188.

THE OTTOMANS

Approximately 200 years after the Crusaders were driven out, the Turkish Ottomans took over the land and have probably had the strongest influence on modern Syria. They brought a certain amount of material success to the land and were Sunni Muslims like most Syrians. They allowed local administration by Arabs who were at least nominally loyal to them. These Arabs were wealthy landowners with deep roots in cities such as Damascus and Aleppo. The Ottomans ruled until the end of World War I, about 400 years.

INDEPENDENCE

After the Turks were driven out of Syria, France and England competed for the spoils. They both had political, religious, and economic reasons for wanting control of Syria.

Syria rebelled against French rule during 1925-1927, but was crushed by superior military power, including a French bombardment of Damascus. The Syrians continued unsuccessfully to fight for their independence until in June of 1945 Article 78 was adopted by the new United Nations. It stated that members of the U.N. could not be placed under occupation by another country. The Arab League declared that the presence of French and British forces in the Levant violated the countries' sovereignty. Finally, after a lot of wrangling and hostilities, French troops left Syria on April 17th, 1946. This is called Evacuation Day, which is today a national holiday.

The Azem Palace in Damascus was the 18th-century residence of a Turkish governor.

The self-interest of European powers and ignorance about the Arab world allowed Greater Syria to be chopped into the countries of Syria, Lebanon, Jordan, and Israel.

Syrians voting in the United Arab Republic.

A DIFFICULT START

Syria started its new life as an independent country with enormous problems. The United Nations had given part of Greater Syria to the Zionist Jews of Europe, in opposition to the wishes of the Arab majority in the area and of the neighboring Arab countries. There was almost immediate fighting between Israel and the Arab states, including Syria.

In addition, Syria's economy was weak. Few roads or railroads were built under the French occupation, and most of the land and the climate of the new country made self-sufficiency difficult. The lushest, most fertile parts of the Levant now formed the new countries of Lebanon and Israel

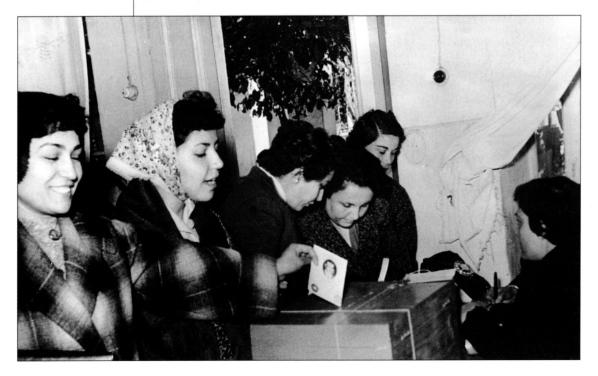

or had been given to Turkey. Despite millennia of being part of technologically advanced civilizations, Syria was now mostly backward and pastoral.

The difficulties Syria inherited resulted in a series of military coups from the very beginning of independence. The threat of military takeover has continued to plague Syria to the present day.

In 1958, Syria and Egypt tried to put Pan-Arabism—the belief that all Arab people should be part of one nation—into action. Pan-Arabism had been an Arab ideal since the 19th century. Their effort at confederation,

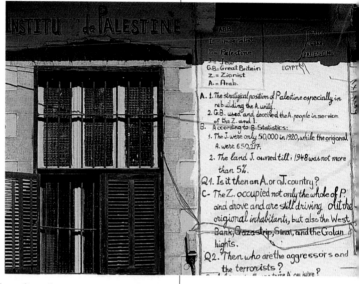

the United Arab Republic, was, however, shortlived. Egypt completely dominated Syria, and the union disintegrated in 1961.

In the mid-1960s, a group of dissident military officers came to power through the growing and powerful Ba'th ("BAA-uth") Party, a Pan-Arab party in Syria and Iraq. The Ba'th Party was founded by two peasants from minority sects, one Christian and one Muslim. In the new nationalism, the uniting factor was not religious belief but being an oppressed Arab. The Ba'th Party itself was strongly socialistic, which appealed to the Syrian masses; they were tired of the Sunni aristocrats who had cooperated with the Ottomans for centuries, enhancing their own wealth and power.

In 1970, Hafez ("HU-fezz") Al Asad, the minister of defense, and troops loyal to him surrounded the Parliament and took over the country in a bloodless coup. He has been in power since, surviving repeated attempts on his life and numerous international crises.

Arguments for Palestinian independence on the front of the Institute of Palestine in Damascus. Syria takes a great interest in the fate of Palestine.

Syria's recent history has been plagued by repeated wars with Israel, which have drained the country's resources, and unrest in Lebanon, which affects Syria.

GOVERNMENT

SYRIA'S OFFICIAL NAME IS THE SYRIAN ARAB REPUBLIC, and its capital is Damascus. All citizens can vote for both the president and the members of the legislative assembly.

GOVERNMENT STRUCTURE

In 1971, Hafez Al Asad ("al asad" means "the lion" in Arabic) was elected president by an assembly of his own choosing. The constitution, established in 1973, gives the president almost total control of the country. Presidential elections are held every seven years.

The prime minister and a cabinet of around three dozen members (the number varies from time to time) are appointed by the president; no legislative approval is required. The People's Legislative Assembly consists of 195 members who propose laws, discuss cabinet programs, and approve the nation's budget. It also has the power to override presidential vetoes by a two-thirds vote but has never done so.

The assembly is the closest thing the country has to a genuinely democratic institution. All adult citizens can vote, and candidates for the assembly need not be from the Ba'th Party. In fact, a varying proportion of members are from outside the party—about one third of them at this time, and quite a few are women. Although the constitution requires that the president be a Muslim, there are no religious qualifications for the assembly. The constitution does require at least half the assembly members to be workers and peasants (farmers and rural workers). Terms of office are four years.

Opposite: **A statue of Asad at Asad Dam. According to official government statistics, President Asad received 99.9% of the vote in the 1991 election; no one has ever run against him.**

Below: **A local government building in Damascus.**

A political banner displays Asad's picture. Even though the government now allows citizens to grumble openly, it tolerates no organized opposition.

THE BA'TH PARTY

The Ba'th Party is headed by a 21-person Regional Command chaired by the president. There are many organizations under the Regional Command: the Revolutionary Youth Organization; the Union of Students; the Women's Organization; the Peasant's Federation; the General Federation of Trade Unions; and groups for journalists, electrical engineers, and just about every economic pursuit. The military has its own branch.

Anybody who wants to succeed in the Syrian government must do it through the Party by showing unfailing loyalty to it and to President Asad. The best jobs in the government often go to people who are from the president's extended family, the same religious group (Alawites), or the same region of the country (the coastal mountains) as the president.

THE LEGAL SYSTEM

Syria's system of justice is based on the French model. There are civil and criminal courts. Lawsuits and other civil cases often take years to settle.

The State Security Court is only for political opponents the government accuses of being "security risks." Trials in this system violate most international standards for fair trials.

Courts governing personal status, such as birth, marriage, and inheritance, are divided according to religion. For Muslims, there is a court that follows the Muslim code, called the *Sharia*. There are separate courts for Druze, Roman Catholics, Orthodox believers, Protestants, and Jews.

THE MILITARY AND DOMESTIC CONTROL

Syria's political system is widely regarded as one of the most autocratic in the world, and its prisons hold a large number of political prisoners. In 1992, however, it was announced that 2,864 political prisoners would be released, thereby raising hopes for a degree of liberalization.

Syria also has a large military. The regular armed forces totaled 408,000 in 1993. Defense expenditures for 1992 were estimated at $1.2 billion, or about 30% of the national budget. A strong military is needed to protect the government; the size of the military is also understandable in view of the fact that Syria and Israel have technically been at war for nearly half a century. In addition, it is estimated that 30,000 troops are deployed in Lebanon, where Syria is deeply involved in maintaining the peace.

All young men are supposed to serve at least $2^{1}/_{2}$ years in the military, but there are exceptions. One is that an only son cannot be drafted; another is to "buy" one's way out of military service. In 1992, the price was $5,000. Although this is a fortune for most Syrians who work inside the country, young men who leave to work in the Persian Gulf, and earn much more than they could in Syria, use this loophole.

Syria has an army and air force but no navy. The presidential guard is a separate force under the command of a member of President Asad's family.

Women may volunteer for military service, and there are special military schools for young women cadets.

A policeman in Damascus. Syria has a large police force.

ATTITUDES TOWARD GOVERNMENT

Bakshesh ("buk-SHEESH," bribe or tip) is common, from paying a traffic officer to avoid a ticket to buying a favor from a party or government official. Smuggling in consumer products is a major industry with bakshesh paid to customs, military, and officials for their assistance.

At gatherings in Syria, politics is often the chief topic of conversation. Most Syrians have a strong libertarian streak and are wary of any government. Particularly in rural areas, people generally believe that the government does not understand their problems. In urban areas, regional jealousies have created tensions with the government. Currently there is a feeling among other groups that the government favors Alawites.

Although the government is unpopular with some groups—mostly the fundamentalist Muslims and the old-time aristocrats—there is a lot of support for it among common people and some religious minorities. The people who support the government are those who have benefited socially, politically, or financially or who feel that secular government protects the diverse religious practices in Syria better than one that imposes religious beliefs as law. While Westerners are sometimes appalled at the lack of certain freedoms, the characteristic of strong, autocratic leaders is thousands of years old in Arab culture.

NATIONALISM AND GREATER SYRIA

Rivalry among the country's various religious and ethnic minorities has been an ongoing source of instability in Syria. National loyalties traditionally take second place to religious and ethnic loyalties, and so the government appears at times to Syrians to represent no more than one more faction among factions. In the years since independence, however, an intense patriotism has developed, along with a strong desire for the recovery of what Syrians feel are integral areas of Syria split off from the nation by French authorities. These areas include Hatay province, which is now part of Turkey, the whole of Lebanon, and the Golan Heights. The return of the Golan Heights, which was taken by Israel in the 1967 war and annexed in 1981, has been a Syrian condition of peace with Israel.

Opposite: **The Golan Heights were annexed by Israel in 1981. All Syrians except Druze were expelled from the area and Israeli settlers were moved in.**

Above: **Pro-Khomeini graffiti on the wall of a mosque. Some Muslim fundamentalist groups oppose the government because it is secular.**

Many Syrians advocate the wider goal of restoring Greater Syria. Greater Syria is considered to encompass present-day Syria, Lebanon, Jordan, and Israel or Palestine. For this reason, Syria has taken a personal interest in Lebanese politics and maintains troops there. Syria has also insisted on being involved in the Palestinian peace process and has offered refuge to numerous Palestinian refugees.

The Ba'th Party also reflects the viewpoint of many Syrians in championing pan-Arab nationalism. It advocates the unification of all Arab countries into one nation that would include all of the Middle East and North Africa. Pan-Arab nationalism regards the borders established by Ottoman or European rulers as arbitrary and artificial and bases its call for unity on the shared heritage of Arabic language and culture.

ECONOMY

SYRIA IS A MIDDLE-INCOME, developing country. Although there is poverty and only a few people are wealthy, the number of middle- and upper-class people has grown in recent years. Government price controls on basic items allow even the poorest people to survive. The country is not rich in oil like countries in the Persian Gulf, but it does produce some oil and is engaged in major exploration for more.

The early 1990s saw greater expansion of the economy, although Western confidence in the economy remains low, and foreign investors are still reticent. Syria's support of Kuwait in the Gulf War of 1990–1991 improved its relations with the Gulf states, which subsequently granted aid for infrastructural and industrial projects, and with the United States and the European Union, increasing the possiblities for economic cooperation.

Twenty years ago Syria was overwhelmingly an agricultural country. Today its economy is divided among industry, mining, and agriculture.

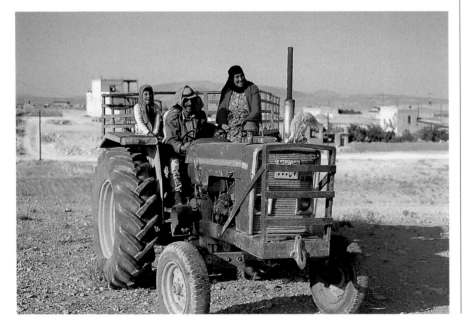

Opposite: **Flaring off gas on an oil pipeline. Transit fees from pipelines have frequently been lost because of political turmoil.**

Left: **A family works together on a farm.**

Threshing grain. Syria has had to import some grain in recent years.

AGRICULTURE

In the 1970s, 50% of the population was involved in farming; in the 1980s this figure had fallen to 30%. Today agriculture employs 23% of the work force and contributes 30% of the gross domestic product (GDP). Cotton, once Syria's biggest export, remains an important part of the economy, along with fruit and vegetables.

Syria is nearly self-sufficient in basic food products. It produces a large amount of chicken and lamb and some beef. Its primary vegetables and fruits are chickpeas, lentils, tomatoes, potatoes, onions, cucumbers, cabbage, beans (both dried and green), squash, eggplant, artichokes, peas, corn, parsley, lettuce, melons, peaches, pears, pomegranates, prickly pears, apples, figs, dates, grapes, olives, and pistachios.

The southwestern corner of the country might be called the nation's breadbasket, because this is where most of the wheat is grown. Tobacco has recently been introduced into this area to augment the wheat, melons, corn, prickly pears, pomegranates, and grapes already produced there.

MINING AND MANUFACTURING

Mining contributes 14% of the GDP. Petroleum alone accounts for almost 60% of total export earnings. The main fields are at Qaratshuk, Suwaydiya, and Rumaylan in northeastern Syria and at Deir-ez-Zor in eastern Syria. Syria also has some phosphates, natural gas, and iron ore.

Manufacturing employs 14% of the work force. However, Syria's industry has been hampered by frequent shortages of power due to insufficient hydroelectric power. Important products include petroleum, coal, rubber, and plastic products, clothing, leather products, footwear, food products, beverages, and tobacco. Textiles are an important part of the manufacturing sector. Locally grown cotton is spun into thread at factories in Aleppo, Hama, and Damascus. Cotton, wool, and other fabrics are manufactured, and silk brocade is made by hand.

EXPORTS AND IMPORTS

Syria's primary exports are oil, cotton (grown mostly around the Euphrates River), vegetables and fruit, and textiles. There is also a growing number of import-export businesses that export such things as food and industrial products. From 1991 to 1993, the country's total annual exports remained about the same: $3.4 billion.

During the same time, imports increased from $2.8 billion to $4.1 billion. The top nine imports for 1991 were: steel pipes used to create modern sewage and drinking-water systems, sugar, manufactured fibers, wheat, wheat flour, yellow corn, rice, chemicals, and soybean meal.

An oil pipeline brings crude oil to refineries in the western part of the country.

Selling fish in Latakia.

JOBS

With few exceptions, Syrians are able to pursue whatever livelihood they choose. One exception is that an engineering graduate must work five years after graduation for a government agency before going into private practice or obtaining a better job with private industry or outside the country. Family and social pressures and economic realities, however, often dictate what career a young person pursues, despite the official freedom of choice.

The difference between the richest and poorest people in Syria is less noticeable than it is in Egypt, Mexico, or even the United States. The monthly salaries of most workers and professionals (without a private practice) range from around 1,500 lira for a janitor to 5,000 lira for a geologist who has been on the job for 30 years. This is the equivalent of about $35 and $100, respectively—not a large difference.

University professors fare only a little better, and even cabinet members' salaries are incredibly low by Western standards. However, it is surprising how well Syrians manage on meager salaries.

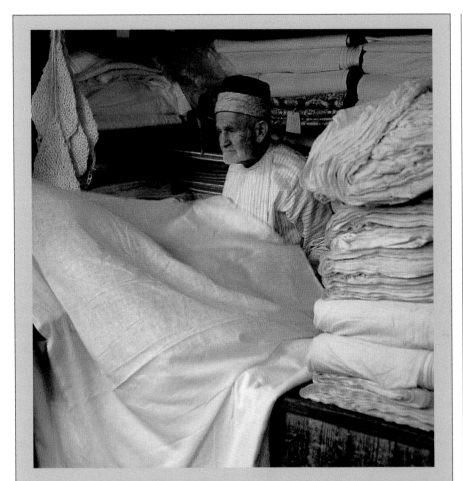

With a little family inheritance, maybe a small shop, and several salaries, families get by. Bus and taxi fares, medical fees, and the prices on locally produced food, clothing, and medicine are among the lowest in the world.

A DAY IN THE LIFE

With such low salaries, how do Syrians survive?

The government has strict rent control laws that help families afford their living quarters. Young people whose families have money assist them until their incomes are adequate. Nearly everyone works at two or three jobs. A man might work as an electrical engineer for the government in the morning, sell electrical equipment to hospitals for a European company in the early afternoon, and work in his video rental store until 9 or 9:30 p.m. Millions of Syrians follow a similar pattern. In additon, many people participate in unofficial currency exchanges with foreigners or smuggling. Finally, families pool their incomes, and young people rarely leave home before marriage (and often for several years after they marry).

OPENING UP THE ECONOMY

From the coup in the mid-1960s up to the mid-1980s, Syria's economy was highly centralized. All utilities, transportation, and heavy industry were owned and operated by the government. Small merchants and crafts workers, professional people, farmers, and shepherds were free to operate their own means of livelihood, but with price controls.

About the time that the Soviet Union—a long-time patron of Syria—began to look for ways to decentralize economic control, so did Syria. Investment Law 10, a 1991 directive issued by President Asad, liberalized economic restrictions and encouraged private investment in certain commercial and industrial areas. The government, however, remains the country's utilities manager, heavily subsidizes public transportation, sets prices on fuel and basic foods, and operates most heavy industries.

The traditional *norias* ("NOH-ree-ahs"), or water wheels, have long provided irrigation to Syria's farmland. Lack of water is a major reason for economic problems.

There are both negative and positive sides to this half-and-half approach. The most obvious plusses are the availability of many basics that used to be scarce (toilet tissue, for example), an expanding middle class, some better-quality products, and the lack of economic and social chaos like that which has plagued the former communist countries. The most apparent disadvantages are that government-run operations are still very bureaucratic and inefficient, there is no modern banking system, and outsiders are wary of investing here.

ECONOMIC PROBLEMS

Although tax rates in Syria range from 17 percent on lower salaries to 64 percent on the highest incomes, tax evasion is widespread, and the profits from smuggling and unofficial currency trading escape taxation. At the same time, the gap between imports and exports is growing. Combine these problems with the huge portion of the country's budget spent on the military, bureaucracy, and secret police (as much as 80 percent), and they add up to a perpetual shortage of money. Syria currently owes around $10 billion in international debt and cannot pay it.

The infrastructure is weak. Syria's bridges, roads, schools, and utilities are inadequate and outdated. The plumbing and phone systems do not work well, and the electricity is off several hours every day because the government cannot keep up with the growing demand created by a burgeoning population and economic development.

Despite these problems, the Syrian economy is growing. In 1991, the GDP increased by 10.9% and in 1992, by 10.3%.

The millet harvest in the Eghlab Valley. Small farm holdings are still largely unmechanized.

New construction and television advertising are booming, and signs of prosperity are everywhere. Unfortunately, poverty, crime, and Western-style materialism are also increasing.

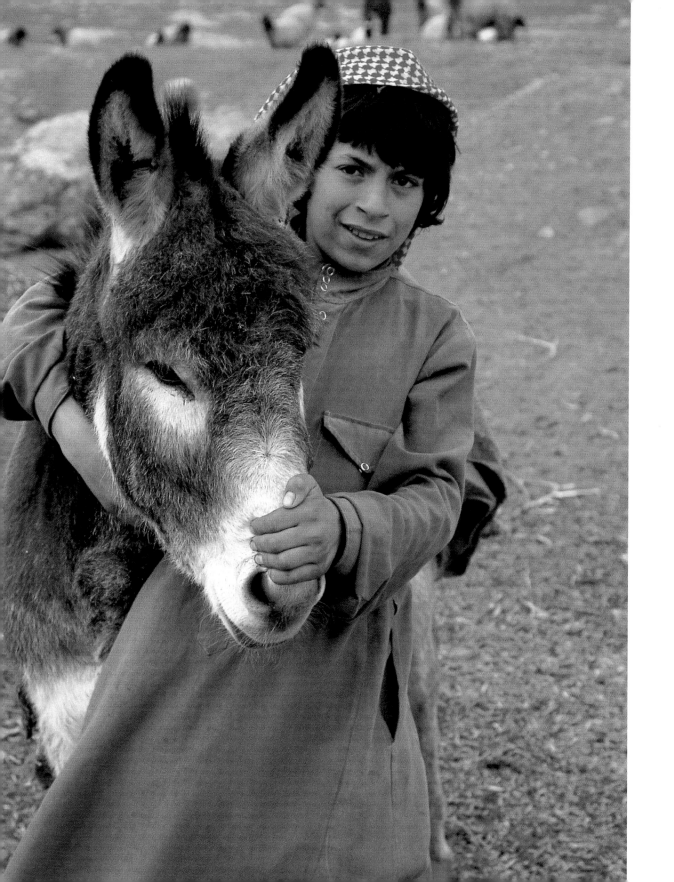

SYRIANS

SYRIA IS A COUNTRY OF extremely crowded cities and mostly unpopulated desert and steppe. Around 80% of the population lives within 80 miles of the Mediterranean coast.

Syria may have the most diverse ethnic mix of any Arab country. Most Syrians are a mixture of ancient Phoenician, Babylonian, and Assyrian and more modern French and Turkish. Most consider themselves to be Arabs.

Although the majority of the people have olive-toned skin, dark brown eyes, and black hair, there is surprising variety in physical attributes. They range from blonde hair and very pale skin to a dark brown skin color with jet black hair. Quite a few Syrians have blue or pale gray eyes, usually with dark hair. Red hair and medium-brown hair are also common—sometimes accompanied by pale, freckled skin and brown eyes.

Opposite: **A Bedouin boy. Perhaps the only "pure" Arabs are the Bedouins.**

Above: **The souk ("sook"), or traditional market, in Damascus. City people are more likely to wear Western clothing.**

POPULATION FACTS

More than half of the population is under 19 years of age. Syria has been one of the fastest-growing countries in the world during the 20th century: at the end of World War I, the population was only 200,000; in 1972 it was 4.5 million; in 1986, 12 million; and in 1993, about 13 million. In 1990, there were 385,000 births and 40,000 deaths.

According to government figures in 1993, Damascus alone had about four million inhabitants. Together, Aleppo, Homs, and Hama add another four million people. This means that most of the country's population clings to the eastern side of the coastal mountains.

VARIED INFLUENCES

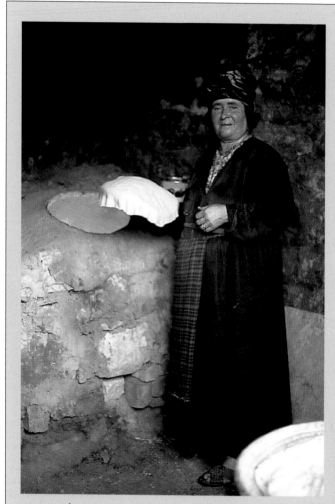

Syrian society includes a variety of social groups of various sizes that lack any set of shared values and loyalties that might bind the population into one nation. Differences in language, region, religion, ethnicity, and way of life produce a large number of separate communities, each with a strong internal loyalty and solidarity. One observer has spoken of the "empty center" of Syrian society, the lack of an influential group embodying a national consensus.

One reason for this disparity is the historical isolation of different groups. Christian groups have always played a prominent role in Syria, especially in the west and north. When the Omayyads first arrived, the various Christian groups, perhaps fearing persecution, moved farther into the mountains, forming separate communities. In later years, minority sects of Islam did the same. Under Egyptian rule, non-Muslim groups were given some autonomy. Under the Ottomans, the practice spread, creating what was called the Millet system: a system that gave Jewish and Christian communities their own governments within the empire.

Religious distinctions are psychologically and politically the most significant ones. Loyalty to one's fellow group members, rather than to the Syrian nation, is an important value. The religious communities are largely self-contained social systems that regulate much of the daily life of their members and receive their primary loyalty. This Christian woman, going about her daily bread baking at the Saint Joseph Monastery, would most likely feel little sense of loyalty to Syria.

In addition, language differences and differences in social organization between villagers, Bedouins, and city dwellers further fragment the society. Each of these represents a distinct, usually hereditary, way of life. Syria's post-independence history is largely the story of conflict between minority groups and the central government.

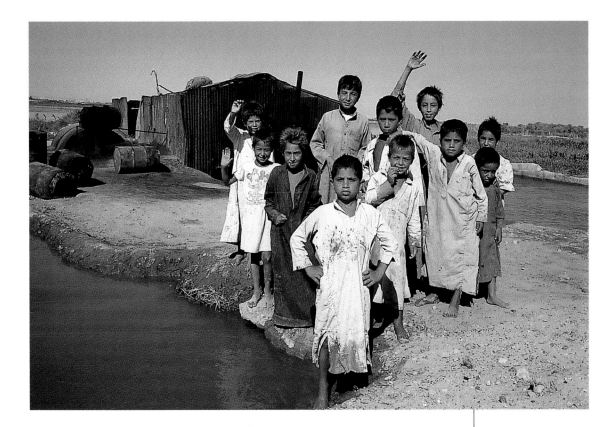

RACIAL AND CLASS CONSCIOUSNESS

In Syria, the lightest-skinned people dominate the top social-economic positions and the dark-skinned people the bottom ones. Top government officials, business owners, and models used in TV commercials are almost uniformly light-skinned and often European in appearance, whereas construction workers, janitors, garbage haulers, and street cleaners are predominantly darker-skinned.

Although there is no violent racism, there seems to be a general feeling of superiority among lighter-skinned Syrians. Blacks are not generally liked or respected, nor are the Bedouins, even though they are the original Arabs whose ancient cultural elements are still a big part of modern Arabia.

Class consciousness is also very real. There is little socializing between upper and lower classes, and the lower classes generally seem humble and accept their status.

Poor rural children. Educated city dwellers feel superior toward illiterate villagers and rural people, and those who live in the cities of the western part of the country feel superior toward those who live in the eastern part.

ETHNIC DIVERSITY

Arabs live in all parts of the country; non-Arab groups generally live in partial isolation from each other, either in their own village or cluster of villages or in specific quarters of towns and cities.

KURDS The Kurds are believed to constitute between three and nine percent of the population. Most live in the foothills of the Taurus Mountains north of Aleppo, in Al-Jazirah, near Jarabulus northeast of Aleppo, or in the Quarter of the Kurds on the outskirts of Damascus. They are a fiercely independent people with a deep pride in their history and traditions. Many arrived from Turkey in 1924–1938, in reaction to the Turkish attempt to suppress Kurdish culture by banning their language.

Kurds now live in the mountain regions of Turkey, Iraq, Iran, and Syria. Since the early part of this century, Kurds have been fighting for the independence of this region, which they call Kurdistan.

Kurds are traditionally nomadic herders and speak Kurdish, an Indo-European language. They are mostly Sunni Muslims.

Kurdish women do not wear the veil and enjoy considerable freedom, working and interacting socially with men. However, they are not encouraged to participate in political activities. In the villages, women prepare food and clothing and bring water to the house. Men build the houses and take care of the animals. All help with the planting.

Dress varies for Kurdish women. Traditional dress for men consists of baggy pants bound at the ankles and worn with a tunic, vest, and cummerbund. They wear a brightly colored turban or yellow fur cap and, traditionally, a curved dagger and rifle. Most Kurds, however, now wear European-style clothing, although the traditional costume remains an important symbol of Kurdish unity, as does the appearance of fierceness.

There are about one million Palestinians living in Syria. Some are second-generation, and others were born in Israel. Palestinians are official residents and hold Syrian passports, but cannot vote. Most have assimilated well into Syrian society.

ARMENIANS Most of the Armenians in Syria arrived as refugees from Turkey between 1925 and 1945. They are city or town dwellers, with three-quarters living in Aleppo and another large group in the Quarter of the Armenians in Damascus. Most villagers in northwestern Syria are of Armenian descent. Armenians belong to the Armenian Orthodox Church or the Armenian Catholic Church. Their language is Armenian, an Indo-European language. They work chiefly in trade, the professions, small industry, or crafts and have a strong economic position, especially in Aleppo. They are the largest unassimilated group and retain many of their own customs, maintain their own schools, and read Armenian newspapers.

TURKS The Turks are seminomadic herders in Al-Jazirah and along the Euphrates River, and farmers in the Aleppo area. Most have assimilated into Arab culture, but some still speak Turkish and retain ethnic traditions.

There are also small numbers of Circassians (descendents of Muslim nomads from the Caucasus), Assyrians, and Jews.

These bright-colored dresses are typical of Kurdish women.

Saladin, the Islamic Empire's most successful commander, was a Kurdish officer in the Syrian army. He eventually became sultan of Egypt and Syria and pushed the Crusaders out of Jerusalem.

Syrian men may wear a headcloth similar to that worn in other Arab countries, or a checkered kafeeyeh.

MODE OF DRESS

It would be hard to find more diversity in dress than there is in Syria. With such a large blend of cultures, every sect of Islam, both Eastern and Western Christianity, and disparate tribes from one corner of the country to the other, the clothing is often a treat for the eyes. A young woman wearing a white scarf and a raincoat (even in the burning heat of summer) can be seen arm-in-arm with her best friend— another young woman in tight blue jeans, with teased hair, heavy makeup, and loads of jewelry. A father in kaftan (a man's gown) and *kafeeyeh* ("ku-FEE-yea," a wrapped cotton headdress) might be walking along with his sons, who are in blue jeans and T-shirts with expressions printed in English on the front. An older woman, draped in black from head to foot, might be with her granddaughter, who is wearing colorful Syrian fashions and earrings the size of small chandeliers. Many wealthy and educated Syrians dress similarly to Europeans or Americans. To add to this mix, every village and tribe of Bedouins has its own particular patterns, hand-embroidered designs, styles, and colors of clothing.

One item that symbolizes not only Middle Eastern dress, but Muslim dress in general, is the head wrap. In Syria, there is an endless variety of materials, colors, textures, patterns, and styles of wrapping for both men and women. They range from elegant and gorgeous to torn, dirty, or sun-bleached.

Middle- and upper-class Syrian women, especially the younger ones, tend to wear bright colors, lots of jewelry and make-up, high-heeled shoes, and long hair teased and heavily sprayed, with "fountains" of hair cascading from the top. Young men of the middle and upper classes almost always have closely-cropped hair, and are also very dressy. Few Syrians wear blue jeans, T-shirts, running shoes, or other such casual attire.

Some things rarely seen in Syria are bare legs above the calf, bare shoulders or upper arms, shorts on adults (men or women), mini-skirts, short hair on women and girls, and long hair or earrings on men.

Average life expectancy is low by comparison to the West (64 for men and 68 for women), despite reasonably good medical care. Heavy smoking, high-fat diets, lack of exercise, and the harsh life of village and desert are the main causes.

Typical women's attire would be a long dress and a head covering.

LIFESTYLE

SYRIANS OFTEN SEEM to be a bundle of contradictions, making them simultaneously fascinating and frustrating. Although they are tremendously polite in their greetings and good-byes, they cut in line, jostle people so that they drop whatever they might be carrying, or terrorize pedestrians with their cars. Some taxi drivers and shopkeepers offer goods and services gratis as a welcome, but others cannot be trusted for a minute. Most people go out of their way to be hospitable, but they also honk their horns incessantly, play blasting music, and talk loudly outside bedroom windows at midnight or 6 a.m.

THE SYRIAN CHARACTER

Syrians love to laugh and joke, eat and talk, and dance. They love noise— loud music, hand clapping, car horns, loud voices—and few of them like peace and quiet at all. The younger ones have a tremendous amount of energy, even when in their mid-20s.

This is a culture that strongly believes in fate, and that belief is reflected in the constant use of the expression *"insha'Allah"* ("in-SHAH-al-LAH," meaning God willing) whenever they talk about the future. It shows up in various other ways as well. They have a fatalistic sense of humor that is apparent in their political jokes. They do not monitor time and schedules as do the time-manic North Americans or Japanese. Being on time does not matter because whatever is going to happen is going to happen anyway!

Opposite: **A visitor to a Syrian village can often see women scrubbing clothes on a washboard (or just with her hands) in a small stream or in a tub of water in front of the house.**

Above: **It is common for men to put their arms around each other.**

53

Syrians are a social people, and their preference for a lot of company starts early.

The overwhelming majority of Syrian men smoke, and an increasing number of women also. Most men smoke the argheeleh *("are-GHEE-lay," a water pipe) even if they do not smoke cigarettes.*

SOCIAL INTENSITY

One thing a visitor to Syria quickly notices is the energy put into personal relationships. It is obvious on the streets and in homes, schools, and offices. When Syrian friends greet each other, their hellos and good-byes seem endless. They ask about each other's families and work and school and health, and where are you going, and can you come have tea or ice cream with us? Then they say good-bye in several ways with various blessings on each other. When they learn English, these habits come through in the new language, and they ask strangers how they are two or three consecutive times.

Along with social intensity comes physical closeness: male friends walk down the street arm-in-arm or holding hands; men hug and kiss other men, sometimes even on the lips; and women do the same with each other. Syrian friends touch each other constantly. Even engaged lovers and older married people often walk arm-in-arm or hand-in-hand, although this is not as common as physical contact between the same genders.

BEING PART OF THE GROUP

Syrians do not like to stand out from the crowd. Clannishness is part of their tradition: immediate family first, then clan or village (sometimes these are about the same), religion next, then nationality. The variety in dress is part of this group thinking—they dress as their group dresses.

Most Syrians do not like anything but their own cuisine. There is little variety in the naming of children. Half the men have the first name Mohammed. Many Mohammeds use their middle names for at least a little distinction. The most common men's names are Mohammed, Ahmad ("AH-mud"), Khalil ("khu-LEEL"), Khaled ("KHA-led"), Yassar ("yus-SAR"), Imad ("ai-MAD"), Samer ("SAA-mer"), or one of a half dozen other common names. There is only a slightly larger variety of women's names.

Some modern Arab scholars lament over their peoples' enslavement to tradition at the expense of innovative and creative thinking.

Syrians typically like to feel part of a group.

Syrians are generally fun-loving people who rarely appear to feel sorry for themselves.

A Bedouin family in front of their tent. Family ties are guarded as a means of preventing loneliness as well as a source of support against the outside world in times of stress or danger. For most women, the home is the center of their lives.

FAMILY ORIENTATION

Families are the absolute center of life in Syria, and this shows in many ways.

One of the first questions a foreigner in Syria gets asked is "Are you married?" Then, if the visitor says yes: "Do you have children?" If so, the Syrian will want to know all about the family. People here cannot understand children leaving home at the ages of 18, 19, or 20 (unless, of course, they get married), and they often make clear their belief that they are better parents than most Westerners—particularly Americans. They point to things such as drug use, teenage pregnancy and suicide, and street kids as evidence that this is so. Most young people cannot imagine leaving their parents' homes when they are teenagers. Although some of them complain about lack of privacy and family pressures, they generally think it is for the well-being of everyone. The idea of putting their aging parents in a nursing home is unacceptable to them. (There are none in Syria). Although there is some child abuse and children are punished harshly at times, children and parents display a lot of affection toward each other.

Getting married and having children is the top priority for most Syrians. Children are so important (especially sons) that fathers and mothers traditionally change their names after the first son is born. If they name the son Yassar, the father becomes Abu Yassar—literally "father of Yassar"—and the mother often becomes Umm Yassar—"mother of Yassar." If no sons are born, the mother usually identifies herself as the mother of the first-born daughter; fathers rarely do this, however.

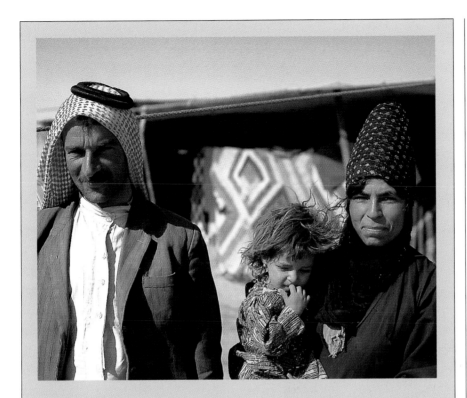

THE PROTECTION OF THE CLAN

Clannish behavior in the Arab world developed from the harsh life of the Bedouins. A hostile environment that required vast areas to support a small amount of life led to the need for a strong sense of survival. An individual alone was vulnerable to both the environment and other individuals or groups.

Therefore the tightest-knit kinship groups thrived the best. A man might kill his cousin or other relative in a feud of some sort, but when family members were faced with any threat (even if only perceived) from the outside, absolute unity was necessary.

It has only been within the past century that most Arabs have become settled and urbanized. Even though many of their cities are thousands of years old, previously only the elite lived in them. For thousands of years, the "law of the desert" ruled, and thus the concept of allegiance to an extended family group became second nature.

This clan loyalty heavily influences modern Arab politics, and who you are related to is more important than laws, money, intelligence, or ability.

Despite the gradual elimination of the Bedouins' lifestyle, many elements of their culture live on, in modified form, in the daily lives of most Arabs: strict segregation of men and women, boys, and girls; arranged marriages; clannishness; submission to a strong and autocratic leader; belief in harsh punishments; a strict code of honor; and warm hospitality.

A Kermany wedding party.

MARRIAGE

Arranged marriages are still very common in Syria, particularly among villagers and Bedouins. Even more modern city people often cannot marry anyone they want; if they want a particular mate, both families usually have to agree on the arrangement. First cousins are still the preferred match. Among more modern Syrians, the father of a young woman may approach a young man he would like to see his daughter marry and ask if the young man is interested. Polygamy is legal for Muslims, although few urban Syrians practice it. Divorce is rare.

THE STORY OF A WEDDING DRESS

Bedouins and villagers are very traditional people. In many Syrian villages, a young woman's marital hopes are often shown by the wedding dress she creates. The patterns of the dresses are set by village or clan tradition, although within those patterns each gown is slightly different. The traditional dress in most northern Syrian villages is heavy black material finely embroidered with scarlet patterns. The dress takes a year or longer to sew by hand and is often signed by the maker: her name is sewn into some part of the garment. The left side of the dress is often highly decorated, while the right side has only coarse, simple designs; this is because the baby is traditionally carried on the right arm. The woman usually wears the dress for several years.

Since marriage is a main goal in life, wedding parties are major social events. Among traditional people, the bride parties with her mother, sisters, female cousins, and friends in a house. They sing, dance, talk, laugh, and eat for hours. The bridegroom does the same with his male friends and relatives. The festivities may go on all night long in the city, all afternoon and evening in a village.

Wealthy people often rent a hotel ballroom or entire restaurant, and after some separate-gender celebration, the whole group may come together to eat, talk, and dance all night.

Depending on the custom of the area, the wedding party might take place either before the actual wedding or after it. Among the most traditional people, the families await the news from the groom, after the wedding night, that the new wife was a virgin. If she was not, or seems not to be, the marriage could be ended immediately and the woman severely punished by her family.

A Western-style white wedding. Weddings are a particularly important occasion for Syrians.

Fathers usually get custody of children in a divorce.

WOMEN'S AND MEN'S ROLES

The constitution adopted at the founding of the Ba'th Party in 1947 stated: "The Arab woman enjoys all the rights of citizenship. The party struggles to raise up woman's level." This position sets Syria apart from most other Arab countries. Women today enjoy full legal rights, and the government has promoted equal opportunities for women. Nonetheless, traditional restraints have prevented most women from taking advantage of these opportunities.

For more than 2,000 years, Arab culture considered women to be inferior and girls to be generally worthless. Women are still viewed as weaker than men in mind, body, and spirit and therefore in need of male protection. The highly valuable and easily damaged honor of men depends largely on that of their women, especially on that of their sisters, so they are carefully protected. The slightest implication of unavenged impropriety on the part of the women in a family or of male infractions of the code of honesty and hospitality could irreparably destroy the honor of a family.

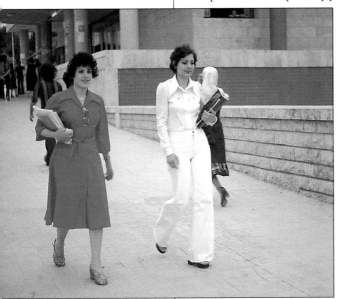

Students at Aleppo University dressed in Western clothing.

Despite traditionally being considered inferior to men, Syrian women today enjoy higher legal status than do women in most other countries of the Middle East. They also have more freedom and are respected more than Western women were only a couple of generations ago. There are women cabinet members and quite a few women in the Peoples' Legislative Assembly. However, fewer than 10% of women work and not more than a handful have positions with any power.

DEATHS IN THE FAMILY

When someone dies, there are three days of mourning, during which time friends, relatives, and neighbors visit the family. Close women relatives are expected to wear black for many months after the death. After a period of time, they can start wearing half black and half white. For very traditional families, it may be a year or longer before the women can wear colors again. For more modern families, the time is usually at least six months. If an older woman's husband dies and she is not likely to remarry, she may wear black for the rest of her life. These mourning traditions are similar in both Christian and Muslim families.

A person (especially a woman) who does not fulfill the mourning traditions is criticized for not having loved the deceased.

A Muslim must be buried within hours, clothed only in a shroud.

Above and opposite:
Schoolchidren going to school. Primary education is compulsory for six years. In 1991, 99% of primary school-aged children were enrolled, whereas only 45% of secondary school-aged children were in school.

EDUCATION

Syria is striving to educate all its citizens, and literacy has increased dramatically in the last 20 years. Syria has one of the highest literacy rates in the Middle East. School children wear green, military-style uniforms and attend school from 6 or 8 a.m. to 1 or 3 p.m. (depending on the season) six days a week. In high school, students are required to study two years of a foreign language, either English or French.

Syria has four universities, and students pay only a token annual fee to attend. There were a total of 170,000 students in Syrian universities in 1994, including some 90,000 at the University of Damascus. However, the universities have huge classes and use outdated teaching and testing methods, so those who can afford to study abroad and can get visas do so. There are also agricultural and technical schools for vocational training.

University students can study whatever they want with this exception: only the top few percent of high school students (based on special exams) are allowed to study medicine, and only the next upper level is allowed to study engineering. Neither group of students has to study in those fields, but they usually do. This creates a situation where the brightest students are most often doctors, dentists, or engineers. And although there are only a few hundred students in the university medical schools, there are thousands studying European literatures.

In spite of compulsory education, the average rate of adult illiteracy in 1990 was 35.5%, which includes 22% of men and 49% of women.

MOSQUE AND SCHOOL

Before there were schools in the Islamic world, there were mosques. Because Islam does not separate any part of life from any other, most Arab countries had no secular (that is, nonreligious) schools until the 20th century. Children were taught by the religious leader, or *sheikh* ("shake"), who assured that their education was based on the teachings of the Koran and the life and teachings of the prophet Mohammed. (One Arabic name for mosque is the same as one used for university: *jaamea.*)

Today in Syria, most villages have secular schools. The few that do not still use a mosque or church school, but the education is usually more focused on modern learning than it was in mosques of the past.

Many traditional Muslim leaders think mosque schools are the best way to assure that young people are taught proper behavior and beliefs. Muslims, however, are not the only religious group that believes this. Where there are large populations of Armenians, there are Armenian Orthodox (Christian) schools that teach children their ancestral history, religion, and the Armenian language; and where there are concentrations of Jews, there are synagogue schools that teach children Jewish heritage and Hebrew.

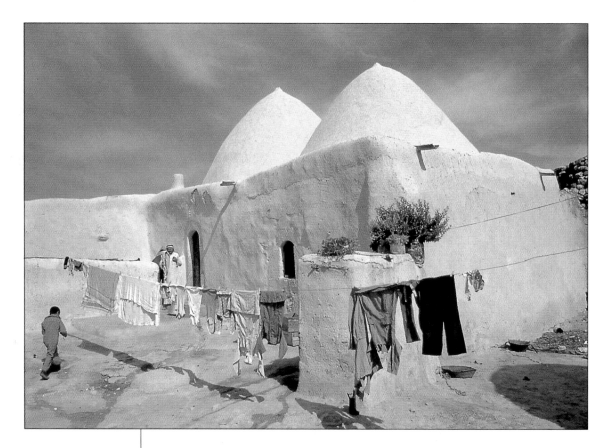

A traditional beehive house in Ebla in northern Syria.

In the more traditional homes, the women and girls sit at one end of the room, while the men and boys sit at the other. If there is more than one main room, the genders may separate completely.

LIVING QUARTERS

All city dwellers live in apartments. Many of them own their homes. Syrian cities have no such thing as single-family homes, except for the mansions of ambassadors and top government officials. Many wealthy and upper-middle-class people build large vacation homes (called villas) in the mountains or near the sea. Some of these are relatively modest, but most are quite extravagant.

The focal point of rural houses is most often the front door. It may be huge compared to the house and is frequently decorated with geometric patterns and painted multiple colors. In the western part of the country, nearly all rural houses are surrounded by olive trees and grapevines. Many houses have grape arbors over the roof to keep the hot summer sun off the house at the same time that it ripens the grapes.

IN A SYRIAN HOME

The styles of decoration and furniture and the sizes of homes vary widely according to social class, religious background, and traditional or modern attitude. If there is a most common decor in the homes of the middle and upper classes, it is a gaudy Louis XIVth style.

The chandeliers and other light fixtures truly stamp a place as Syrian. Many chandeliers are oversized for the rooms they light, sometimes hanging down below head-level. The brass frames are smothered with pieces of multi-faceted glass that, seen from the streets at night, often fill an entire window. Other lamps and light fixtures tend toward the ornate as well: brass floor lamps shaped as palm trees; table lamps glazed in pearlescent black or white with flowers, dolphins, or other decorations in brass-covered relief. All of this ornateness usually rests on colorful French, Turkish, or Persian carpets and multicolored stone floors.

Interior of a Muslim house in a rural area. It is common to sit on pillows on the floor, although there will also be other furniture.

Many of the newer houses and those recently renovated lean toward modern European styles, accented with some Syrian embellishments. At the other end of the age spectrum lie the once grand houses of the ancient walled city of Damascus. These are hundreds of years old, each built around a courtyard with a fountain, grapevines, citrus, eucalyptus, and other trees and flowers. The ceilings are high, the better to keep rooms cool during summer days.

The old section of a city houses the groups that have been there the longest and other groups oriented toward traditional life. The souk *is an important feature of the old city.*

A busy street in Damascus.

CITY LIFE

Half of the population of Syria lives in cities. Cities are composed of several distinct sections. The ancient core of a city may go back to the pre-Greek or pre-Roman period, with sections added in Greek, Roman, and medieval times. Cities also have a more modern section, frequently built by the French, that houses families more closely identified with modern technology and values.

Cities were traditionally organized into ethnic and religious residential quarters. Members of the different faiths still tend to live together, and the quarter functions as a small community within the larger urban setting. A residential quarter traditionally had its own mosque or other religious structure, shops, and coffeehouses where the men met, as well as a *mukhtar*, or mayor, who represented the group to the outside society. Within the quarter, family connections, personal reputation, and honor carried more weight than wealth.

Today many of the wealthier families of the various quarters live in the modern parts of the cities, where neighborhoods are divided along economic lines rather than by religious or ethnic affiliation. As a result, the old quarters have lost some of their leadership, and the division between more traditional-minded people and the modernized middle classes has been accentuated.

VILLAGERS

Although more and more people from villages are finishing high school and even attending college, basic village life in Syria has not changed a lot over the centuries. Villages have less wealth than the cities, there are relatively few cars, and the ancient Arab cultural attributes are more noticeable than in the cities. Villagers' lives are closer to those of the Bedouins than they are to those of city dwellers, and they are less accustomed to foreigners and are more conservative. These traits are especially found in villages in the desert and along the Euphrates River.

Most Syrian villages have electricity, some indoor plumbing, schools, and clinics, but these amenities are not universal. Where there is no official school, the local mosque or church serves as one.

In villages and rural areas, most people live in small, one- to three- room homes with a small courtyard, the older ones generally made from adobe bricks and plaster. Each village has a few villas built by villagers who have made it good in the city or by local farmers who have been successful.

Village life is traditionally based on family and clan, summed up by the folk saying, "My brother and I against my cousin; my cousin and I against the outsider."

Although you might think that camels and Arabs are inseparable, there are few camels in Syria. The most common work animals are donkeys, horses, and mules.

67

Bedouin women produce beautiful and often elaborate carpets, clothing, and jewelry. Now even the full-time nomads usually have to augment their income from sheep with the sale of these craft items.

A Bedouin family in front of their tent.

BEDOUINS

Like indigenous people (the first known inhabitants of an area) throughout the world, the traditional lifestyle of the Bedouins has changed a great deal and will probably disappear soon. This is not the result of colonialism, as it has been with most other indigenous peoples, but rather it is the result of the encroachment of modern living.

The traditional Bedouins' entire existence revolves around raising sheep and herding them from one sparse feeding ground to another in millennia-old seasonal cycles.

There are now three types of Bedouins: settled, seminomadic, and fully nomadic. The settled Bedouin live at the edge of the steppe or desert where there is enough water for them to grow crops. Seminomads winter in villages, then spend the rest of the year grazing their sheep. The fully nomadic groups live in their black goatskin tents all year, moving whenever they must to provide grazing for their sheep.

Two factors are destroying the traditional nomadic lifestyle. The first is modern technology in the form of trucks and tankers that haul sheep to market and water to sheep, circumventing natural watering holes and "sheep drives" to market. The second factor is the control that the government of Syria has gained during the last half-century over the tribal feuding and warfare that were common among clans for

A DIFFICULT LIFE

An elderly Bedouin who goes by the name Abu Ghazi (father of Ghazi) told a journalist from *The Middle East* magazine:

"Fifty years ago there were no cars or trucks, only camels; people lived on barley bread, dates, yogurt, burghal (bulgar), and dried pomegranate seeds. We were living on the bounty of God. We were happy.

"I'd like an easier life, with a nice house, a warm bath, central heating and all; but in the city I wouldn't be able to afford more than a sandwich and a pack of cigarettes."

Another Bedouin talked about the difficulty of life as a desert nomad:

"Bitter water. Dust. It's hot in summer, cold in winter. Scorpions. We have to go 20 kilometers to find drinking water. What kind of life is this?"

thousands of years. Now, instead of fighting with each other and keeping sheep to a level that allowed quick mobility, the Bedouins try to raise much larger flocks of sheep. In a fragile environment, these practices have caused severe overgrazing and have diminished the ability of the land to support sheep.

In the spring when grazing is good in the desert and steppe, Bedouin tents are everywhere; and parked beside most of them is not a camel, but a large sheep-hauling truck and maybe even a generator. Many tents have televisions that run off the generator or truck. Children are often bussed to village school.

A Bedouin family. Women play a full part in Bedouin life, caring for the animals and setting up and dismantling the camps.

Population growth and climate change have also contributed to the demise of traditional Bedouin life. Better health care has increased their lifespan at the same time that the land supports less life. Young Bedouins often end up in villages or cities where they farm, do construction work, clean streets, or do any other work they can find.

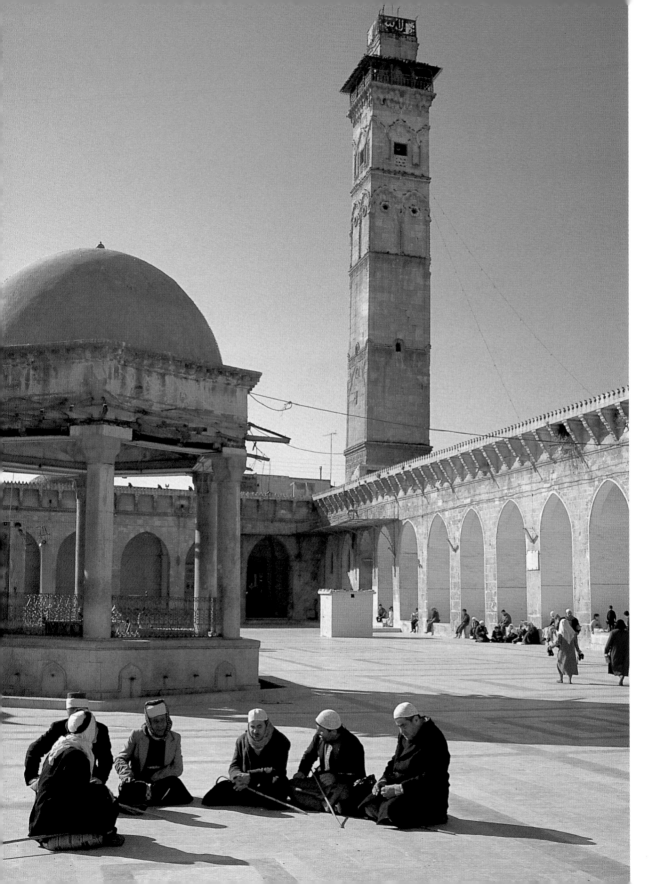

RELIGION

ALTHOUGH SYRIA HAS A LARGE assortment of religious groups, including Muslim, Christian, and Jewish, they all share a strong belief in God. Syrians' greetings, goodbyes, and many other common expressions give credit to God for everything, thank God for everything, and leave the future up to God. The most common response when you ask someone how he or she is, is *"al Hamdulla"* ("al-HAM-dool-la"), which means "Thank Allah!" When Syrians learn English, they translate these expressions into the new language as "God bless you," "God willing," "Thank God." Although some of this may be only tradition without real feeling, it is hard to imagine most Westerners using similar expressions with such regularity. Religion is part of everyday life in Syria, and most people wear their beliefs proudly.

There are hundreds of churches in Syria, and all religions are guaranteed freedom of worship by the country's constitution. Syrian laws do not allow proselytizing—trying to convert others to your own religious beliefs. Perhaps for this reason, there has been less religious strife in Syria than in other countries with similarly diverse populations.

Muslims constitute more than 80% of the population. Of these, 80–85% are members of the Sunni sect, 11% are Alawis, and approximately one percent are Ismailis. Shi'a groups constitute less than one percent of the population. Druzes, an offshoot of Islam, account for three percent of the population, and Christians for 10%. There are also small groups of Jews and Yazidis, a sect that combines elements of Judaism, Christianity, and Islam, as well as older religious beliefs.

71

A spring goddess from Mari, now in the Aleppo Museum.

ANCIENT RELIGIONS

Before the Muslim Omayyads conquered Syria in the eighth century, there had been many religions in the land. The Phoenicians, Assyrians, Babylonians, Greeks, Romans, Jews, and Christians all spread their own particular beliefs in different parts of Syria. The ancient beliefs were eventually replaced by the monotheism (belief in one God) of Judaism, Christianity, and Islam.

BAAL: WHOSE GOD WAS HE?

The name Baal ("BAY-el") was first used in approximately the same sense Christians now use the word "Lord." Many gods were referred to as Baal among the Semitic people of the Middle East: the Sumerian god of the air, Enlil; Marduk, God of Babylon; Asshur, god of Assyria; and others. An Arabic expression for a polytheist—one who believes in more than one god—is *ashra baalla* ("AHSH-ra BAAL-la," literally 10 gods). The Phoenicians initially used Baal as a title for their god of storms, Hadad, but it later became his name. *Baal* is an old word in both Hebrew and Arabic that means "husband," "master," and "owner." Baal Zebub, the healing god of Ekron, later became one word—Beelzebub—which came to represent evil and idolatry in the New Testament of the Bible.

One Canaanite myth claimed that Baal reigned during the growing season of the year, then died thereafter. His place was taken by Mot ("mote," meaning death), god of death and sterility, who represented the hot, dry summers. Anat, who was Baal's wife and sister, searched for him during the reign of Mot, found him, and brought him back from death. That is how the autumn rains began.

Although the Hebrews purportedly believed only in *Yahweh*, they often adopted other "baals" from the Canaanites. One example is Jezebel, the Phoenician wife of King Ahab of the Hebrews.

THE BEGINNING OF ISLAM

Although Judaism and Christianity are native to Greater Syria and have been there for thousands of years, Islam filled the land not only with its beliefs but also with the language of its holy book—the Koran—within a hundred years of its inception.

In 570 the Prophet Mohammed was born to an Arab noble family in Mecca, an area that was then called the *Hejaz* ("hi-JAZ"). He spent most of his life as a merchant, but when he was 40 years old and in solitary meditation, he was visited by the angel Gabriel. The angel began giving him God's words—in Arabic—which eventually became the Koran. He began spreading this new "revelation," attracting both followers and enemies among the people of Mecca. Hostility and persecution from the Meccans eventually forced him and his followers to flee to Medina in 622. This migration marks the beginning of the Muslim year. For eight years, Mohammed headed Islam from Medina, returning to Mecca in 630. Although he died two years later and was buried in Medina, Mecca became the most holy city of Muslims and the Kaaba Mosque its most holy place.

Early Islam was intensely expansionist. Conquering armies and migrating tribes spread out of Arabia. Syria was among the first countries to come under its sway; by 635, Muslim armies had conquered Damascus.

The mosque is the center of religious life for Muslims.

73

Koran school. Religious leaders guide others, but have no special authority.

Islam imposes an ethical code encouraging generosity, fairness, honesty, respect for the elderly and those in authority, and forbidding adultery, gambling, usury, and the consumption of pork, blood, and alcohol.

ISLAM

Today, around 85% of Syria's population is Muslim. Most of these are Sunni Muslims while the rest are Shi'as, Druze, Alawites, and Ismailis. "Islam" means "submission to Allah." Muslims consider their religion to be a continuation of Judaism and Christianity, with Mohammed as the last of the prophets and the Koran (also called "The Book") superseding all other revelations from God. In the Koran, Muslims and Jews and Christians are all referred to as "children of the Book."

Muslims believe in Christ (as a prophet) and in his teachings that are not "superseded" by the Koran. They think it is blasphemous to believe that God, an all-encompassing spirit, could have a human "son." Instead, they believe that Christ's claim to being the son of God is figurative.

Unlike Christianity, where virtually all sects and varieties have an official, universal leader, Islam has no such hierarchy. Each mosque has its holy man—called a sheikh—who holds his position as spiritual guide by virtue of his study of Islam and his perceived piety.

THE FIVE PILLARS OF ISLAM

The Koran and the teachings of and examples set by the Prophet guide every aspect of Muslim life. Everything from government to commerce to life's daily rituals and details are covered. The most prominent religious principles, called the Five Pillars of Islam, are as follows:

1. *Shahada* ("sha-HAA-da"): the declaration that there is only one God and that Mohammed was his last prophet.

2. *Salat* ("sa-LAAT"): prayer five times daily—at sunrise, midday, afternoon, sunset, and evening. The supplicant must face Mecca, and women must cover their hair and entire bodies (except the face, in some sects). (The picture shows a group of men praying.)

Throughout the Muslim world, chanted calls to prayer are broadcast from all mosques and become part of the rhythm of life. Before electricity, a *muezzin* would mount the steps of the minarets (mosque towers) and issue the call. Now the calls to prayer are recordings broadcast over loudspeakers. The chanting is still hauntingly beautiful.

3. *Zakat* ("za-KAT"): an annual tithe of 2.5% of earnings above basic necessities. This is used to build and maintain mosques and help the poor.

4. *Sawm* ("soom"): fasting during Ramadan—the ninth month of the Islamic year.

5. *Hajj* ("haaj"): the pilgrimage to Mecca, with a stop in Medina to pay respects at the Prophet's grave. This is required once in a lifetime, but only if the person has the financial means to do so.

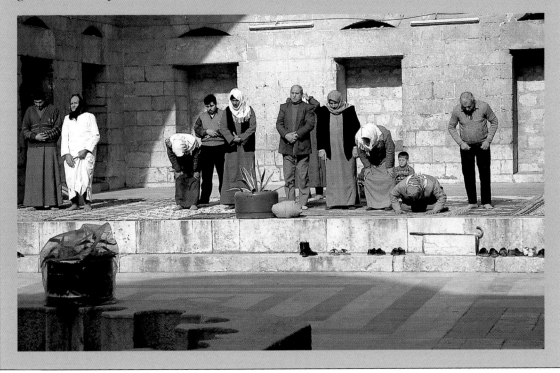

ISLAMIC SECTS AND OTHER GROUPS

Syria's largest religious minority is the Alawis, who number about 1.4 million. They live mainly along the coast in Latakia province, where they constitute over 60% of the rural population. The Alawis are descendents of people who lived in this region in the time of Alexander the Great. Gradually they became influenced by Islam and Christianity. Although today they claim to be Muslims, conservative Sunnis do not always recognize them as such. Like Christians, the Alawis celebrate Christmas, Easter, and Epiphany and use sacramental wine in some ceremonies.

Because many of the tenets of the faith are secret, Alawis have refused

A group of Druze men. The Druze originally came from Lebanon; some remained there and others migrated to Syria.

SUNNI AND SHI'A

The bulk of Syrians belong to the Sunni sect, with a small number of Shi'a Muslims. These two sects are the result of a schism in Islam that occurred in the seventh century. After the death of Ali, the Prophet's son-in-law and fourth successor, or caliph, there was a disagreement over who should succeed him. Muawiyah, the governor of Syria, proclaimed himself caliph, beginning the line of Omayyad caliphs, who ruled from Damascus. The *Shiat Ali,* or followers of Ali, refused to recognize his legitimacy and established a dissident sect that became known as the Shi'a. They believe that the caliph must be descended from the Prophet. The major faction of Islam, the Sunni, believe that the caliph should be elected. This amounts to a division between partisans of leadership by consensus and partisans of divine right.

Today the Sunni sect includes the majority of Muslims around the world. The Shi'a sect is centered in Iran and Iraq, where Ali moved his capital. Syria, the homeland of the Omayyad caliphs, is overwhelmingly Sunni.

to discuss their faith with outsiders. Only a few of their number learn the religion after a lengthy initiation. Only the men take part in worship.

The Alawis formerly were the poorest of the religious groups, and for this reason they tended to join the armed forces in large numbers. They are now the largest group in the military. Since Asad became president, they have become more privileged, and this has caused much resentment among other Syrians.

The Druze community constitute three percent of the population and form the majority in the Jabal al Arab (formerly Jabal ed Druze), a mountainous region in southwestern Syria. The Druze religion is a 10th-century offshoot of Islam, but Muslims view the Druze as heretical. The Druze have always kept their doctrine and ritual a secret to avoid persecution. Only those who demonstrate great piety and devotion are initiated into the mysteries. The initiated are a very small minority but may include women. Although women are veiled in public, they are permitted to participate in the councils of elders.

The Ismailis are an offshoot of Shi'a Islam, the result of a disagreement over the Seventh Imam. There are around 200,000 Ismailis in Syria. Originally settled in Latakia province, they now live mostly south of Salamiyah on land granted to their community by a sultan of the Ottoman Empire.

Orthodox priests. The 19th-century election of an Arab patriarch of Damascus to replace the Greek patriarch in Constantinople has been described as "the first real victory for Arab nationalism."

CHRISTIANS

The major Christian sects in the country are Syrian Orthodox, Greek Orthodox, and Armenian Orthodox. There are also quite a few Roman Catholics and a handful of Protestants and Russian Orthodox. The Syrian Orthodox Church still celebrates Mass in Aramaic, the ancient language of Christ. Christians account for about 10% of the religious population. Christmas and both Easters—Western and Orthodox—are official government holidays.

Most Syrian Christians live in or near the coastal mountains. A drive through the mountains reveals many villages with a church or two but no mosques. These mountains also contain numerous monasteries and convents, some very old as well as some new. Christians are more often city dwellers than Muslims; many live near Damascus, Aleppo, Hama, and Latakia. They tend to be well educated and relatively affluent, working more often in the professions.

With the exception of the Armenians and Assyrians, most Christians are Arab, sharing the pride of Muslims in the Arabic tradition.

CAVE PEOPLE

At the beginning of Christianity, most of what is now Syria was part of the Roman empire. The Romans were tolerant of the religions of the people they conquered, as long as those people did not threaten the empire and at least gave occasional sacrifices to Roman gods. Much later, Christian belief was outlawed and made a capital offense.

Christians were secretive and aloof, would not serve the empire in any way, and engaged in practices that made nonbelievers suspicious. This led to increasing persecution during the second and third centuries. Thousands of Christian believers escaped to the eastern side of the coastal mountains and lived in caves to hide from their persecutors. Just outside Damascus, there are many cave houses carved into hillsides, sometimes high up where they can only be reached by ladder.

The largest concentration of caves is in Maalula, north of Damascus and close to the modern border of Lebanon. Hundreds of cave houses were carved into the limestone cliffs here, and the people even buried their dead in a cave cemetery!

In the modern village of Maalula, houses have been built over some of the caves and have incorporated them into the living space.

Although there are a few dozen synagogues, most Syrian Jews have emigrated in the last few years. Only a few hundred remain, but they too can observe their own religious practices.

LANGUAGE

ARABIC IS A SEMITIC LANGUAGE along with Hebrew, Aramaic, Syriac, and other ancient tongues of the Middle East. Arabs have a rich oral tradition, and according to some Arab scholars, the oral mastery of even illiterate desert and village Arabs is extraordinary. The use of language is the supreme Arab art form.

The differences between Arabic and English are so great that native speakers of one who become fluent in the other often continue to have trouble with the very different rhetorical styles. These differing styles are at the heart of the cultural gulf and the often incompatible views of life that divide Arabic- and English-speaking peoples.

HISTORY

Arabic is ancient—its roots go back thousands of years; and because of its holy status in the Koran, it has probably changed less over the last thousand years than any other major language. Arab traders spread Arabic into Africa and India hundreds of years ago, and languages of both those areas bear some similarities to Arabic. Somali and Swahili in particular contain a lot of Arabic-based words.

A fair number of English words originated in Arabic. Some examples: alcohol, algebra, check, checkmate, lute, magazine, mosaic, safari, Sahara, sheriff, shish kabob, and tariff. The numerals used in Europe and North America were also originally Arabic. Syrians, however, now use numerals that came to them from India.

Opposite: **Two people writing in the mosque.**

Above: **Journals are published by government ministries and other official bodies or by religious or professional groups.**

DIFFERENCES IN USAGE

Native English speakers have developed the linguistic and cultural values of understatement, precision, use of logic, and brevity. In other words, say what you mean very clearly, and no more. Native Arabic speakers, on the other hand, have developed the cultural and linguistic values of emotional appeal, overstatement or exaggeration, repetition, and words in lieu of action.

EMOTIONAL APPEAL Some Arabist scholars (scholars who study Arab culture) have claimed that Arabs are swayed more by words than by ideas, more by ideas than by facts. Educated native English speakers might be impressed and their thinking influenced by a logical argument loaded with facts and figures; an Arab—either educated or illiterate—will most often be impressed and won over by powerful emotional arguments.

This difference creates a communication barrier. A typical educated native English speaker has little respect for an emotional appeal, thinking that it shows bad taste or is a sign of weak thinking, whereas Arabs feel the cool, detached, fact-filled arguments of a Westerner lack something human.

OVERSTATMENT AND REPETITION Writing style also varies greatly between English and Arabic. Compared to typical American writing, Arabic is flowery, wordy, and repetitive. Arabic writing often says the same thing over and over in slightly different ways.

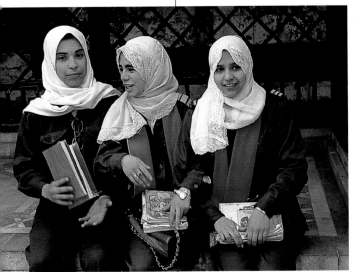

Schoolgirls engage in a quiet conversation.

Arabic does not use a present tense form of the verb to be. *For example, the Arabic sentence* Ana modarres *("AH-na mo-DAR-ress") translates literally into English as "I teacher."*

Overstatement is also used for politeness. If you say *marhaba* ("MAR-ha-ba") or *ahlan* ("ah-LAWN")—hello—to a Syrian, the answer will usually be *marhabtain* ("mar-hab-TAIN") or *ahlain* ("ah-LAIN")—two hellos—or *ahlan wa sahlan ("ah-LAWN-wa-sah-LAWN"),* hello and welcome. In other words, the response outdoes the initial greeting.

WORDS INSTEAD OF ACTION Another characteristic of Arabic that is foreign to most native English speakers is the use of threats without action. If Syrians make a threat, they are unlikely to carry out the action. However, people from a culture where idle threats are not often made perceive the threat as real and act accordingly.

The converse of this trait is that when Arab enemies (perceived or real) say nothing, that is the time to worry. In Arab villages and among nomadic tribes, "honor" and vengeance killings, though now illegal, often take place with no warning at all when a family feels it has been dishonored.

A grand gesture while bargaining at the market.

Arabic verbs are quite hazy about time; the basic forms are past, nonpast, and imperative. In the Koran, there are verses in which Allah did something in both the past and future at the same time.

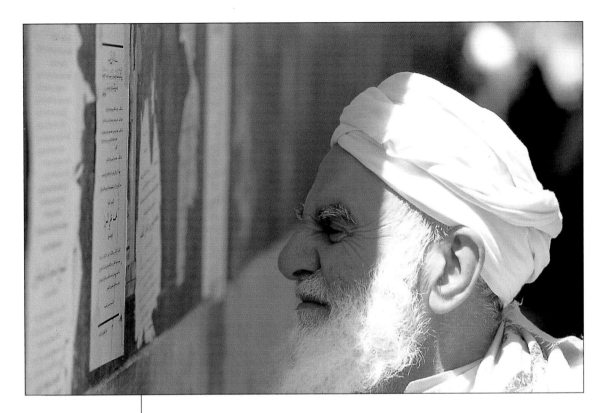

A man reads notices in Arabic. All speakers of Arabic, Persian, and a few other languages use the same alphabet.

Arabic is spoken by 100 million people.

ARABIC DIALECTS

Spoken dialects are far more diverse than are worldwide English dialects; so much so, in fact, that a Damascene has trouble understanding an Egyptian, and an Omani and a Moroccan can understand very little of each other's speech.

The differences in dialects are not only in pronunciation and intonation, but in the use of different words. A Syrian shopping for vegetables in Morocco would find that familiar produce has a different name; the Moroccan would not understand the Syrian words for the vegetables. The Egyptian dialect is well known for using a lot of words that are different from other dialects.

Even from city to city, there are noticeable variations; and the farther apart the cities are, the greater the difference. The dialect in Deir ez-Zor (on the Euphrates River) is quite different from that in Damascus, a little more than 300 miles away.

SOME ARAB PROVERBS

One who has no good for his family has no good for any other.

Marriage is fate and destiny. (Meaning: It is not necessary to marry the one you love.)

Halime returned to her old habit. (Meaning: Human beings can't change themselves, and if they try they will fail.)

Throughout its lifetime, the tree never reached its God. (Meaning: Don't be too ambitious; be content with what God has provided you.)

What has been written on the forehead, the eye will see. (Meaning: What has been ordained by God will happen sooner or later.)

Whoever marries my mother will be my stepfather. (Meaning: I will obey and respect anyone who has higher status or is more powerful.)

A narrow place can contain a thousand friends. (Meaning: When people love each other, they can fit into a tight place.)

Feed the mouth, the eye will be shy. (Meaning: If you "tip" someone, he will not hinder your business.)

Where there are no people, there is Hell.

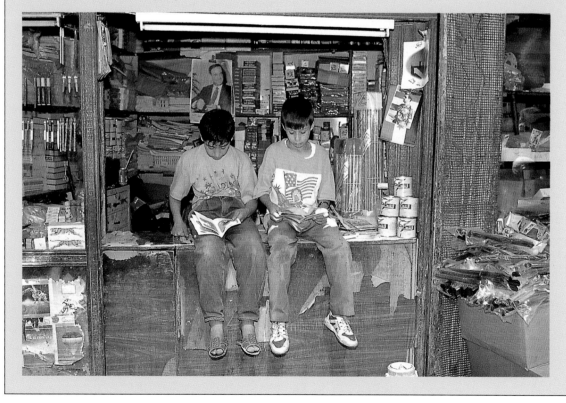

WRITTEN ARABIC

The Arabic used today for most kinds of writing and certain types of formal speaking is classical Arabic, which is the language of the Koran. Classical Arabic is the same for all speakers of Arabic regardless of region. With the increase in literacy in the Arab world, classical Arabic is becoming more widely known, and some Arab thinkers and leaders hope that eventually it will replace local dialects.

A Koran bookshop. The Koran is the standard for classical Arabic.

Arabic is written and read from right to left. There are no capital letters, but many letters change form depending on their position in a word. In addition, there are several different styles of writing that use different shapes for some letters.

The ancient style of written Arabic is extremely elaborate and decorative and difficult to read, even for most Arabs. The style used in newspapers and magazines, called modern standard Arabic, is easier to read except for someone learning the language. The reason is that the marks indicating short vowels (there are both short and long vowels) and double consonants (there are both single and double consonants) are not used in modern writing. Without these symbols, it is often difficult to know what word a person is reading. Imagine, for example, reading English with all short vowels omitted: "pen," "pin," "pan," and "pun" would all be spelled "pn!"

THAT'S A MOUTHFUL!

There are several Arabic sounds that have no equivalent in the English alphabet. They are as follows, showing the English letter or letters usually used in transliteration (writing a language with the alphabet of a different one):

H (*ha*): a heavy *h* sound.

kh (*kha*): similar to the *ch* sound in German *Bach*; the back of the tongue against the rear roof of the mouth doesn't completely block off the air flow.

S (*sahd*): a loose-tongued *s*; the tip of the tongue is not against the ridge behind the upper front teeth, but the front part of the tongue is flat against the front of the palate; somewhere between *sh* and *s* in English.

D (*dahd*): a loose-tongued *d*, same instructions as for *sahd*.

T (*taa*): a loose-tongued *t*; same as above.

Z (*zaa*): a loose-tongued *z*; same as above.

9 (*ayn*): a vowel formed with a narrowing of the throat; a lot of difference in intensity of this sound between some dialects.

Street signs in Arabic. The Arabic alphabet developed from a form of Aramaic. The oldest record in Arabic dates from the fifth century B.C.

gh (*ghayn*): like a *g* without the back of the tongue actually touching the roof of the mouth; sometimes sounds like *l* or *r*.

' (*hamze*): a glottal (voice box) stop; like someone in the Cockney dialect would say bottle, *bo'le*; the way most western Americans say *t* when immediately followed by *n*: important, *impor'ant*; button, *bu'n*.

q (*qaa*): a stop like a *k*, but made in the throat; Syrian dialect substitutes *hamze* for this.

BODY LANGUAGE

When Syrians talk to each other, they stand close and use lots of hand gestures. They tend to speak loudly, as well. Such things are likely to make a newcomer think a fight is about to start, but this is not the case. Even what in the West would be considered an aggressive stance—standing close and leaning toward another person—is normal here.

Two men talking in a park. Syrians tend to sit close together when talking.

There are some head movements that Syrians use to communicate. A quick upward movement of the head with raised eyebrows, often accompanied by closed eyelids and a click of the tongue, means "no." A downward nod to one side means "yes." Shaking the head from side-to-side (like an American saying "no"), often accompanied by a puzzled look, means "I don't understand," or "I didn't hear you."

Hand gestures here are similar to those in Greece and Italy. Holding the palm turned up with fingertips together forming a tent over the palm while pumping the hand and forearm means, "Wait a minute." Holding the arms out to the side and raised as if to catch raindrops with the palms up and open means, "What's going on here?" Drawing the open hands up quickly above the shoulders, palms facing the other person, means, "That's my point," or "That's my excuse." Brushing the open palms together quickly as if to brush off dirt signifies, "I'm finished with it (or with you)."

Another common gesture is patting the right hand over the heart when meeting someone. This shows affection for the person.

OTHER LANGUAGES

The most popular and widely spoken foreign language in Syria is English, with French a close second. After English and French is German, then Russian. Most educated people speak at least a little of one of these—students in high school are required to study a couple years of either English or French. Most Syrians who speak another language live in Damascus. Rural areas and villages, particularly in eastern Syria, have few people who speak anything but their own Arabic dialect.

Some ancient languages are still alive in Syria: in Maalula and the surrounding area (an hour's drive north of Damascus), Aramaic—the language Christ spoke—is still used; in the far northwestern corner of the country, the Armenian language is so common that signs are in both Arabic and Armenian; there are a few speakers of Syriac (one of the original languages of Syria) and of Kurdish in the northeastern part of the country; some people in the north speak Turkish; and some Jews can speak or at least read Hebrew.

The earliest records of Aramaic go back to 800 B.C. in northern Syria. It is now spoken only in small enclaves in Syria.

89

ARTS

ART IN MODERN SYRIA mostly takes the forms of language, music, fabrics and other handicrafts, and jewelry. The designs, materials used, and even colors are most often determined by tradition rather than imagination.

EARLY ART

Syria's museums contain sculptures and ceramic art spanning many thousands of years. Most of the ancient art was related to function—things such as fertility goddesses, vases, and fighting shields. The majority of art in these museums is Roman sculpture and remnants of mosaic floors. The Roman art here is Byzantine (eastern Roman Empire) and differs noticeably from that of the western Roman Empire (Europe).

Opposite: **An artist painstakingly paints an intricate design on wood.**

Left: **An Assyrian bas-relief from the Aleppo Museum.**

LITERATURE

Syrian culture is a part of the Arab whole. In order to escape government censorship, many Syrian writers have moved to Beirut, which has become the publishing center for the Arab world. These writers see themselves as representing the entire Arab world rather than just Syria.

Syria has inherited a rich tradition of Arabic literature, in which poetry is a particularly important form. Public recital of odes was a common feature of Bedouin life, and the public reading of poetry continues to be part of Arab life.

Adunis has had an especially wide influence. He was born Ali Ahmad Said in 1930. He was influenced in his early days by the ideal of Syrian nationalism. At about this time, he took his pen name, Adunis, which was the name of the mythical god of Syria who died in winter and was resurrected in the spring. As a student at Damascus University, he questioned both literary conventions and the social and political structure of Syria. He was imprisoned and then exiled to Beirut in 1956, where he has remained since.

Adunis maintains that only radical change in all aspects of life will bring the Arabs into the 20th century. He uses poetry as a means of inducing revolutionary change to create a new society. In his search for revolutionary poetry, Adunis has developed a language that is allusive, evocative, and mystical—and often difficult to understand.

One of the most popular of contemporary Arab women writers is

In *New Noah,* Adunis sees the poet as a second Noah, searching for a new life and a new god:

Our appointment is death
Our shores a despair we are used to
A frozen sea of iron water we are content with
We cross it moving to its end
We move across and do not listen to that God
We long for another new lord

Ghada al-Samman, who was born in a Syrian village in 1942. She studied English literature in Damascus and London and then moved to Beirut. She went on to work as a journalist, poet, and novelist. Samman shares the preoccupations of many male writers—identity and loss of self, hatred of the harsh and unsettling social and economic conditions of the time, the tension between tradition and modernity—but she also writes of the alienation she feels because of her femininity and her intellect.

In *Gypsy Without a Haven,* a woman speaks to her lover who is apart from her. He is married and she is engaged to be married to man her family approves of. Unable to decide whether to conform to tradition or to break away, she longs to lose her identity in that of her lover, but also longs to conform: "Two men are struggling for her. One wants to give her a home. Her mask loves the home and she wears it in order to bring a smile to the faces of those she loves. . . . The other man only has for her a new tale of wandering. And she is content with that because a home is accidental and exile and sadness are the reality of human existence now."

"Contemporary Arab writers have been preoccupied with themes of struggle, revolution, liberation, emancipation, rebellion, alienation. A writer could not be a part of Arab society and not concern himself with change."

—Halim Barakat, Syrian writer and sociologist

ABU'T-TAYYIB AL-MUTANABBI (MUTANABBI)

Mutanabbi is considered to be the last great classical Arab poet. Of Kufan origin and Syrian apprenticeship, he died in 965. No one else contributed so much to the common stock of quotations in Arabic letters:

> Honor the man of noble soul, he becomes your slave.
> But the mean-souled man when honored grows insolent.

> Whoso desires the ocean makes light of streams.

> Naught will suffice for the understanding of men
> When the light of day itself stands in need of proof.

The oud, an ancient stringed instrument that is the ancestor of the European lute, is popular in Syria.

MUSIC

Arab people respond in similar manner toward both language and music, and there are many similarities between the two. The language is repetitive and exaggerated, and so is the music; the language is rich in subtleties, and so is the music; and the language is rich in storytelling tradition about honor, family, and love, and so is the music.

Arabic music is unlike any other, and dramatically different from western music. Western music uses half and whole notes and often makes great jumps in the music scale; Arabic music uses a lot of quarter notes and makes very small jumps on the scale. The music sounds somewhat baroque—highly decorative—like the music of Bach, although without as much variation on the music scale.

There are two types of native music in Syria. Classical music uses the oud, the flute, and small, lap-held drums, sometimes without a lot of vocal accompaniment. Modern music uses an orchestra of mostly European instruments with one lead vocalist and a back-up chorus.

Arabic music has had a heavy influence on other music around the Mediterranean, Africa, and in southern Asia, due to the Arab Empire of the eighth to 10th centuries. Indian music, for example, has a similar texture, rich in quarter notes, and Spanish flamenco music is a direct descendant of classical Arabic music.

ARCHITECTURE

Islamic art finds its greatest expression in its mosques. The Omayyad Mosque is one of the most important buildings in the whole of Islam. A former Byzantine church dedicated to Saint John the Baptist, the mosque was built on the site of an old temple consecrated to the Syrian god Hadad that later became the temple of Jupiter Damascenus. Rebuilt in 705, the mosque has walls lined with marble overlaid with golden vines and a wooden roof inlaid with gold, while from the ceiling hang 600 gold lamps. It is the finest example of the Omayyad art that spread from Damascus throughout the Muslim empire and was a major influence on the rest of the Muslim world.

The Citadel of Aleppo is probably the greatest military edifice of the Middle Ages. The present building was built in the 12th century by the Mameluks. The souks of Aleppo, which cover 15 miles, date from the 16th and 17th centuries and are considered to be some of the most beautiful in the Orient.

The Azem Palace was built in 1749 as the residence of one of the Ottoman governors of Damascus, Assaad Pacha El-Azem. It is considered to be one of the finest examples of 18th-century Arab architecture.

Since Islam forbids representational art in its mosques, Syrian decoration has concentrated on intricate geometric and floral patterns. The mosaic tile work of the mosques is particularly impressive. Calligraphy, or decorative writing, is also used frequently in Islamic art.

Sayyida Zainab Shit mosque in Damascus.

A shop selling hubble
bubble pipes in a variety
of colors.

HANDICRAFTS

Many Syrian handicrafts are unique to the country, at least in special designs and details.

JEWELRY Syrian gold and silver work is extravagant. Bedouins have a centuries-old tradition of making elaborate jewelry for women, and this tradition is evident in modern jewelry. Middle- and upper-class Syrian women wear lots of jewelry: huge, sparkling earrings that often look like small chandeliers, large rings, and lots of bracelets, some meticulously filigreed. These are made from gold, brass, or a gold-tone metal; the educated city dwellers are very class conscious and do not wear silver. It is the Bedouin and village women who wear silver, and most antique Bedouin jewelry is silver. Bedouin women and some village women also wear jewelry in or on their head covers and veils, in the form of delicate chains and coin-like decorations.

Elaborate silver teaspoons, cocktail forks, trays, and baskets are also made by jewelers.

CARPETS THAT POINT

When Muslims pray they face and bow toward the birthplace of the Prophet—Mecca, which is in northwestern Saudi Arabia. The supplicants always pray on a carpet. The floors of all mosques are covered with carpets, and people who are praying elsewhere use a special prayer carpet. Some of these small rugs, such as the one shown here, are made completely by hand by Bedouins. Many have arrowhead designs woven into them; when the carpet is laid down for prayer, the arrows are pointed toward Mecca.

OTHER METAL WORK Brass and copper plates, bowls, and pitchers are common and lovely. The copper work is disappearing, though: it was a tradition of the rapidly dwindling Syrian Jewish population. There are also water pipes and large coffee servers (samovars) made from filigreed brass and copper.

WOODWORK Another Syrian specialty is mosaic woodwork. There are two basic types: one uses thin layers of factory-made veneers; the other has the wood, bone, or mother-of-pearl cut and set by hand. The crafts workers who do the latter can be seen in their shops, painstakingly cutting and fitting the tiny pieces.

There is wide variation in the quality and design of mosaics. Some inlays have only different-colored woods, while others contain bone or mother-of-pearl (most of it now artificial). There are boxes of every shape and size, trays, tables, game boards ranging from lap-size to large table-top models, and even desks made from mosaics.

Damascus has always been famous for its mosaics. The different elements of the mosaic are not inlaid individually. Instead, a bundle of lengths of various woods cut in the desired shapes is stuck together. Thin slices are then sawn off and placed on the item to be decorated.

Some examples of Syrian creativity in glass design.

FABRICS The fabric arts in Syria take the form of clothing, tablecloths, pillow covers, and carpets. Most carpets made here are created by the Bedouins on horizontal, hand-built looms. The large ones are used to cover the floors of their tents, and small ones are used as prayer rugs. Particularly beautiful rugs are hung on the walls.

Traditional garments, such as dresses, capes, jackets, and various sorts of gowns (for both men and women) with a great variety of embroidery, are still made by Bedouins and village people. Syria has a thriving clothing industry. The clothes tend to be brightly colored with an amazing profusion of designs—especially men's shirts and women's clothing. Here Syrian creativity seems completely uninhibited.

DAMASCENE STEEL

During the Middle Ages, sword makers in Damascus became famous all over the Middle East, central Asia, and southern Europe for their swords. Through a lengthy and arduous process these weapons were made so sharp they could cut a floating spider web, so hard they could cut the shaft of a spear, yet so flexible they could be bent 90 degrees and spring back to a perfect shape. The secret alloy from which the swords were formed was called Damascene steel.

But these were more than weapons: they were works of art. Through a process called Damascening, the handles were incised with elaborate patterns. The cuts were then inlaid with bronze, gold, and silver.

In the 14th century, one of Damascus's many conquerors carried off all the sword makers and put them in his own service, and the art of Damascene steel soon died out. The process of inlaying, however, lives on even today in elaborate and intricate workmanship in both metal and wood.

Tablecloths and pillowcases with unique Damascene designs are now embroidered by machine but are still intricate and striking in appearance.

There is a special brocaded fabric known as *damask* ("DA-mask"), named for Damascus. The original damask, developed hundreds of years ago, was made exclusively from silk (Damascus was on the ancient Silk Route between China and India and the West) interwoven with silver and gold threads. Crusaders brought it back to Europe in the 11th century, where it became popular. Some contemporary damask is still made from silk, but many other types of cloth are also used. It is still made by hand.

What makes the fabric special is not only its elaborate and elegant designs, but the weave, which creates a raised pattern on both sides of the cloth—perhaps the world's first reversible material.

GLASS Yet another Damascus specialty is handblown glass. There are two ancient glass factories that make glass in three different colors: cobalt blue, green, and amber-brown. Each color is produced for a month, another color for another month, on endless rotation.

The objects range from small tea glasses and bowls to large, brightly painted vases, light fixtures, and hubble bubbles (water pipes). In between are various sizes of bowls, glasses, cups, ashtrays, and decorative pieces.

The prayer wall of Omayyad Mosque in Damascus shows the influence of Damascene steel.

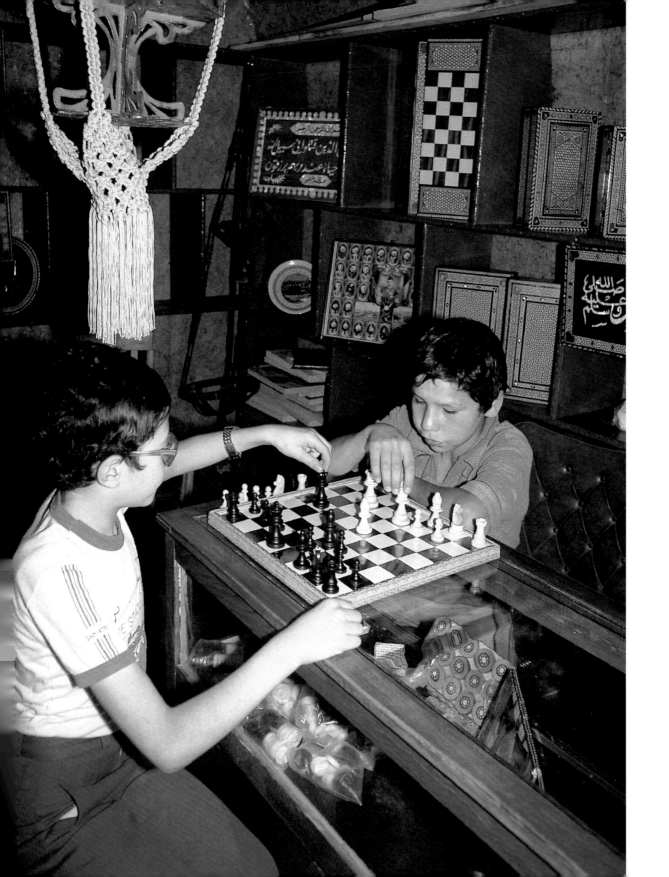

LEISURE

SYRIA IS NOT RICH in leisure-time activities and the people do not have much free time anyway (most of them work eight to 10 hours a day, six days a week), so eating and socializing are the main forms of entertainment— the only ones in rural areas and villages. Syrians love to talk, and they can do it endlessly, often with an entire group talking all at the same time.

MEN THINGS AND WOMEN THINGS

Social activities generally involve either whole families, only men, only women, or women and children. Some public activities are socially unacceptable for women.

Many older men sit around for hours at the all-male tea houses, drinking tea or Turkish coffee, smoking the hubble bubble (water pipe), and either talking or playing Syria's favorite board game—a Turkish variety of backgammon. Even men who are tending shops spend their time doing these things when there are no customers. On Thursday nights (the beginning of the weekend), young men swarm the streets, just hanging out, looking at young women (who are almost always with their families) and talking; or if they have cars, they cruise the streets.

Women, on the other hand, are usually on the streets only with their parents, husbands, and children. Most often, though, they are home working or shopping for their families while the men are on the streets socializing. Their leisure time is mostly limited to chatting with other women or family members.

Opposite: **Children playing chess. Chess is an ancient game that may have originated in the Middle East.**

Below: **Bedouins drinking hot tea. Socializing over a cup of tea or coffee is the main leisure activity for Syrian men.**

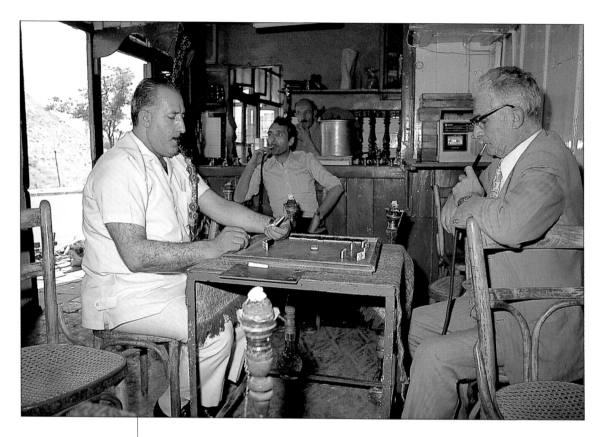

Businessmen playing a board game in an Aleppo coffee house.

SOCIALIZING

Lunch and dinner with friends or extended families are often major social events, with restaurants full until after midnight, particularly on Thursday evenings. During the warm months—from about May through October—dining is usually under the stars, since most restaurants are either partially or completely outside. Depending on the work people do, either lunch or dinner is the big meal of the day. Whichever it is, they often spend two or three hours socializing, eating, and drinking tea. Long dinners are especially common in the cities.

On Fridays during nice weather, many Syrians who have cars drive to nearby mountain resorts where they spend the day doing the same things they do in the city: eating, talking, and strolling the streets. The mass of people and the traffic jams in Bloudan, a wealthy resort in the mountains between Damascus and Beirut, are phenomenal on Friday evenings.

When Syrians go out to walk around the streets and parks at night—something they do in hordes during nice weather—they wear their best clothing. Even conservative Muslim women often wear fashionable scarves and dresses. Young people parade around for a potential marriage partner. In the summer, ice cream shops are particularly "hot" places, much like the old soda shops in the United States.

For natives who have money to spend, shopping is a favorite pastime and part of the nighttime socializing.

On warm evenings, city parks are jammed with people. Children play in the playgrounds while adults talk, and a few young lovers even get to hide from the prying eyes of parents for awhile and hold hands, hug, and (if they are daring) kiss.

Relaxing in a bath house in the Damascus souk.

CHATTING, GOSSIPING, TEASING, AND MORE TALK

The favorite pastime for Syrians is talking. They never seem to tire of it and it fills most of their leisure time. Men sit in coffeehouses and discuss politics over a cup of coffee or tea and a hubble bubble, while women stay at home and chat with family or neighbors. The art of conversation is well developed, and people are respected for their wit and humor.

Men like to engage in a kind of structured teasing, a verbal game of seeing who can come up with the most ingenious way of needling his opponent. An important aspect of the game is inventing an insult that is both clever and eloquently expressed. These verbal displays are rooted in the long tradition of boasting rhetoric in classical Arabic poetry.

MOVIES, CONCERTS, AND GALLERIES

Many city dwellers spend hours every evening watching television. Those who speak other languages like to watch the multilingual channel from Damascus, which has nature and science shows, English, French, and Russian movies, cartoons, and comedy shows. Most other local and regional channels broadcast only in Arabic and show Egyptian, Lebanese, and Syrian soap operas that are often quite melodramatic.

Except for an occasional Hollywood drama, cinemas show soapy Egyptian or super-violent American and Asian movies. These are attended exclusively by rowdy young men. A rare exception to this situation is the international film festival held in Damascus in the autumn of each year, when films from many countries are shown.

The more affluent Syrians own VCRs, and for them video rentals are a source of entertainment that is second only to socializing.

Educated city dwellers like concerts, and Syrians love music in general. Concerts range from classical European to classical Arabic to American jazz to Indian.

Syria has a National Symphony that performs two annual concerts at a new performance hall outside Damascus, and the hall is usually packed.

A cinema in Damascus showing Egyptian movies.

SPORTS

Syria has a soccer team and a basketball team, both of which play in a Middle-Eastern/African league. However, there are far fewer sports fanatics than in the United States and Europe. The games are sparsely attended, and only a few hours a week of television time is dedicated to sports. Not only are they not sports spectators, but few Syrians engage in athletic activities or exercise of any kind.

A few people hunt birds (all over the country) or foxes and gazelles in the desert, but this is more for food than for "sport." Fishing is also rare and done primarily either for food or as a job.

Some Syrians who live near Lake Al Asad use the lake for fishing and recreation. Swimming on hot days and playing in small rowboats are the main activities.

In recent years, Syrian women have become involved in sports, participating in various competitions.

BATH HOUSES

Hammams ("hah-MAM"), or bath houses, are remnants of the Ottoman Empire. They are found in the oldest sections of the cities and are common gathering places for middle-aged and older men. As with coffee houses, men are likely to smoke their hubble bubbles here, while relaxing and enjoying a good conversation.

FESTIVALS

SYRIA DOES NOT HAVE A LOT of celebrations, and most it does have are religious. Chief Muslim holidays are *Eid al-Fitr* ("ah-EED al FIT-ur") at the end of the fasting month of Ramadan, and *Eid al-Adha* ("ah-EED al AD-thah") at the end of Hajj (the pilgrimage to Mecca). Christmas and Easter are celebrated by Christians, but there are not many community festivities for these holidays. Christians usually have a quiet family celebration for holidays, although some decorations appear in shops around Christmastime.

Important anniversaries, which reflect the sense of national identity following independence, are Revolution Day on March 8, the Birth of the Arab League on March 22, Martyrs Day on April 6, the commemoration of French withdrawal on April 17, and the National Day of Mourning on November 29.

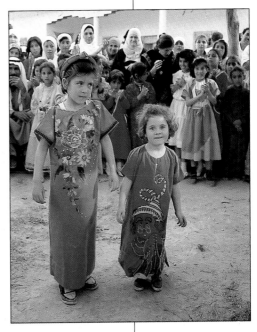

Opposite: **A festive crowd at the pillar of Saint Simeon Stylites.**

Above: **Two small girls share the limelight at an impromptu celebration.**

MAJOR SYRIAN HOLIDAYS

"Variable" means the holiday is based on the lunar calendar.

New Year's Day	January 1
Revolution Day	March 8
Western Easter	variable
Eastern Easter	variable
Evacuation Day	April 17
Eid al-Fitr	variable
Eid al-Adha	variable
Islamic New Year	variable
The Prophet's Birthday	variable
Christmas	December 25

MUSLIM FESTIVALS

All Muslim festivals vary in date from year to year. The Islamic calendar is based on the phases of the moon, and so has only 354 days. This means that the major festivals occur 12 days earlier each year compared with the calendar used in the United States and Europe. The dates for Eid al-Fitr and Eid al-Adha are determined by the sighting of the new moon and so occur at different times in Islamic countries that are distant from each other.

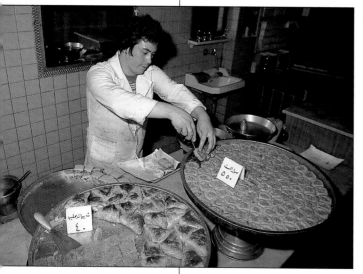

A pastry shop in Aleppo. Special foods are part of the Ramadan celebration.

Alawis celebrate Christmas and Easter as well as Muslim holidays.

RAMADAN Ramadan is the ninth month of the Islamic calendar. During Ramadan, Muslims fast from sunrise until sunset. From the first light of day until the imam can no longer distinguish between a white and a black thread in natural light, Muslims refrain from eating or drinking. This can become difficult if Ramadan falls during hot weather, and young children, the elderly, the sick, travelers, soldiers, and women who are menstruating are excused from fasting, although they must make it up later. People often become very tired during the fast, and life generally slows down. Ramadan is a time for Muslims to focus their attention on spiritual matters, and many families put aside time to read the Koran. The act of fasting proves their devotion to Mohammed and Allah. It also builds self-discipline and instills compassion for those less fortunate.

The celebration comes with the evening meal (called *iftar*) that breaks the day's fast. Food is set on the table in vast quantities, and the family is seated and ready to attack the food at the broadcasts from the minarets that mark the end of the day's fast. Once the eating starts, no one says anything for awhile, and unlike regular meals, which often drag on for an hour or more, the food is gone in minutes!

Iftar is made special not only by the hunger that builds up during daylight hours, but by special foods, the sheer quantity of food, and the frequent presence of extended family.

Eid al-Fitr Eid al-Fitr is the "breaking of the fast" that immediately follows Ramadan, and people gorge themselves on special foods (especially sweets), stay up all night, and spend their time visiting extended families and friends. People traditionally wear new clothes during Eid. It is also customary for children to get money from their uncles. For a poor uncle in a typically large Syrian family, this can be a large burden. Carnival-type rides for kids are set up in large parks, and young people ride horses and go-carts around the parks and pop firecrackers in the streets. Eid is officially only three days, but if those days fall midweek, some shops, schools, and embassies close for the entire week.

Eid al-Adha Eid al-Adha is celebrated in about the same manner as Eid al-Fitr. It comes at the traditional end of Hajj, the pilgrimage to Mecca, and celebrates the near-sacrifice of Ishmael (who is called Isaac by Christians) by his father Abraham. During Eid al-Adha, almost nothing is open—government or private—the streets are nearly deserted, and this is the only time the cities are relatively peaceful and quiet.

Muharram ("moo-ha-RAM") is the Muslim New Year, and marks the day Mohammed and his followers set out for Mecca on their flight from Medina. It is celebrated quietly with the family.

Shoes for sale in the souk in Aleppo. It is traditional to buy new clothes for Eid al-Fitr.

Festivities at a wedding.

OTHER CELEBRATIONS

WEDDINGS Reflecting the supreme importance of family in Arab culture, weddings are perhaps the most extravagant events and the biggest celebrations in Syria. Suppose you are in a Syrian city, walking around late one night, and you hear the sounds of a drum, clapping, and chanting male voices. You look around to find its source and see a couple of men leading the chants, white skull caps on their heads, standing on the shoulders of others who are walking in circles. This a traditional Muslim wedding party. While the men

MAKING A PARTY

Life in Syria is quite simple compared to the West, but this does not mean that Syrians do not know how to have fun. The opposite is true, in fact. Nothing seems to make a group of Syrians happier than "making a party," the English expression they often use. All it takes to get them going (especially the younger generations) in almost any place and at almost any time is some music, some sweet treats, and cola—the name they give all soda drinks, regardless of flavor. They clap and sing along with music, and it is usually only a few minutes before some of the men get up and start imitating the movements of a belly dancer. Arab women do not belly dance in front of men, at least not in public, but the men do. And they love it. They laugh hysterically at each other's attempts to "shake their booties" and bounce their breasts. They "make parties" on picnics, in restaurants, and in the city parks. They get so carried away at times that they dance on restaurant tabletops! Everybody talks at once, and they completely lose themselves in the celebration—a spontaneous festival.

When students go by bus on field trips, they start singing and clapping early in the morning and keep it up, off and on, all day.

are performing this ritual in the street, the women are in a nearby restaurant or home dancing (often belly dancing for each other!), singing, and feasting. When the women finish eating, the men eat, and the party lasts most of the night.

Less traditional people with lots of money usually rent the ballroom at a luxury hotel and eat, drink, and dance all night.

FOLK AND MUSIC FESTIVALS Each September, an international festival is held in Busra, in its amazingly well-preserved Roman amphitheater that seats 15,000 people. The festival runs every night for approximately three weeks and has many international folk dance and music groups. There are also occasional folk dance and music festivals in Palmyra, Aleppo, and other cities. These performances attract more foreign residents and tourists than Syrians, however.

Just prior to the Busra festival, there is a regional festival of sports, music, dance—just about everything—at Sports City (a newly-developed stadium complex) north of Latakia on the coast.

There are quite a few government-related holidays, sometimes accompanied by fireworks exploded on Mt. Qassioun ("qa-see-OWN"), the small mountain near Damascus. Some have parades, military aircraft shows, and Ba'th Party speeches.

FOOD

HOSPITALITY IN THE ARAB WORLD is as old as Abraham. Visitors to Syria are often surprised at the invitations they receive to visit the homes of locals they barely know or to have tea with a shopkeeper or a stranger in a village. This characteristic is not only religious in origin but is ingrained in the Arab code of honor. Honor, in various forms, is critical to Arab people, and to be inhospitable, even to enemies, causes dishonor.

Meals, especially those eaten with friends or visitors, are a major source of social life and entertainment. Tea or coffee and appetizers can last a long time. A meal is likely to last two hours at lunch, three hours or more at dinner.

Muslims do not use their left hand when eating, since the Koran dictates that the left is to be used for toilet functions. It is traditional for the host to insist that the guest eat more until everything on the table is gone.

Syrian cuisine is similar to that of other Middle Eastern countries. Some dishes have become popular in the rest of the world. Hummus, an appetizer made by blending sesame paste and chickpeas, and tabouleh, a salad made of bulgur mixed with tomatoes and parsley, are familiar Syrian dishes. Felafels (patties made of ground chickpeas) have also made their way into Western countries, as well as the flat round breads called pitas. Baba ganouj, a mashed eggplant dish, is another emigrant.

For Syrian Muslims, certain food restrictions apply. Islam forbids the consumption of pork or alcohol, and meats must be specially prepared (called *halal, or "hah-LAL,"* cooking).

Opposite: **A fruit shop in the souk.**

Above: **A man carrying bread in the courtyard of a mosque. Bread usually accompanies meals.**

A special party held 10 days after the birth of a child includes a special drink called koralya, *which is made from sesame seeds. It is not drunk at any other time.*

INGREDIENTS

Whether served at home or at a restaurant, Syrian food uses essentially the same ingredients: lots of lamb, chicken, dried beans (especially chickpeas), eggplant, rice, and bulgur (cracked wheat). Additionally, olives, yogurt, and Syrian cheese (a white, usually salty cheese most often made from goat's or sheep's milk) are commonly part of meals. There are dozens of varieties of olives, ranging from enormous to tiny, from yellow to jet black, from bitter and dry to sweet and juicy, and from crunchy to soft. Garlic and olive oil (or purified butterfat) are also used heavily in or on most foods. Coffee or tea follows every meal.

SWEET AND SOUR

Syrians love food that is either intensely sweet or intensely sour. The country has one of the highest per capita consumptions of sugar in the world, and the soft drinks are the sweetest in the world. Even Canada Dry sodas and 7-Up that is bottled under license in Syria are sweeter than in Greece, just a few hundred miles away. Syria's own brands are sweeter yet. The traditional Arab sweets, too, are so sweet a person can only eat one or two small pieces. On the other hand, the pickles are extremely sour, and people like to eat sour, unripened fruits and nuts.

Here are some food practices in Syria:

• Most food is eaten by hand or picked up or scooped up with bits of flat bread, but french fries are eaten with a fork.

• French fries are the only form of potatoes eaten, and they accompany every restaurant meal.

• All flat bread dips are drizzled with olive oil and garnished with fresh parsley or mint.

• Syrians eat all parts of an animal—brains, gonads, and intestines.

DAILY MEALS

For those who eat breakfast, it often comes quite early—school days start at 6 a.m. during the heat of summer, and devout Muslims get up before dawn to pray. Lunch, the largest meal for most people, is around 2 p.m. and is followed by a siesta. Except for special occasions, dinner is usually light and always eaten late; in fact, most restaurants do not open until 8 p.m. and stay open until midnight or later.

Meals range from a light breakfast of olives, cheese, yogurt, and Turkish coffee to special family dinners with dozens of dishes. The main meal consists of soups (lentil is a favorite), stews made from chicken or lamb, salads, appetizers of various sorts, different kinds of stuffed pastries, cooked vegetables, bread, and fruit for dessert. They are nearly always accompanied by trays of olives and very sour pickles. A late supper might include olives, cheese, yogurt, bread, and tea.

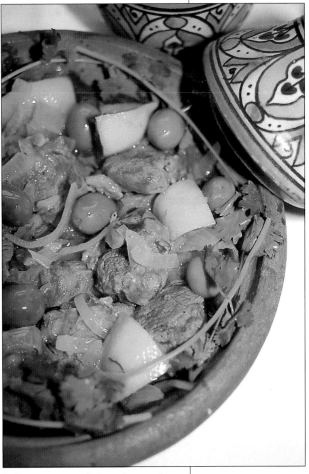

Lamb and lemon stew is a typical main meal.

Syrians make some special foods—a few in large enough batches to last most of a year. One such item is small eggplants stuffed with spiced meat and then pickled. Small zucchini-type squash is also stuffed with a rice-meat mixture but not pickled. Yet another favorite is artichoke hearts stuffed with spicy meat and pine nuts.

IN THE KITCHEN

Syrian kitchens of the middle- and upper-classes are similar to but not as elaborate as middle-class American kitchens. Few Syrians have such luxuries as dishwashers, food processors, microwaves, and meat grinders. Poorer Syrians—which is most of the population—get by with basic utensils and a lot of hard work in the kitchen. For example, garlic is bought in large bunches and first chopped then crushed in a mortar and pestle. All this work falls to the women of the family, particularly the mother, because few Syrian men cook or even know how to.

Rural women baking bread in a clay oven.

HUNTING AND GATHERING

Most groceries are bought fresh every day. In modern families, the whole family may share the shopping chores. This is almost necessary because not many Syrians have cars and the quantity of food needed by a large family is vast.

Shopping for food in Syria is time consuming, because there is a separate shop for each type of food. There are even four different types of bakeries: one bakes only flat bread, a Syrian staple; another bakes baguettes and sandwich rolls; another creates elaborately decorated European-style pastries; and the fourth makes Syrian specialties—dense, rich confections with heavy use of pistachios and sugar water.

In addition to larger shops, there are many streetcorner kiosks that sell candies, toiletries, magazines, and newspapers. In some neighborhoods, fresh local produce can be bought from farmers who trek through with their donkeys or horsedrawn carts, chanting their lists of goods.

Shops in Syria sell narrow ranges of goods and are often clustered into special *souks*. One goes to a grocery store for packaged and canned goods, a fruit stand for peaches and apples, a vegetable stand for carrots, one butcher shop for chicken and another for beef, and so on.

In very traditional Muslim families, the father and sons often do all the shopping because they do not want the women out on the streets.

117

A street kitchen offers some traditional dishes.

Most dinners end with Turkish coffee or strong tea served in small glasses.

DINING OUT

Syrian food is the same whether it is in Aleppo, Damascus, or Deir-ez-Zor. The only difference is that some dishes vary slightly in texture, flavor, and spiciness. Standard dishes are grilled lamb or chicken; a Syrian specialty called *kibbeh* ("KIB-beh," a delicious meat pie made with ground lamb, bulgar, pine nuts, and seasonings); *boorak* ("BOO-rok," a cheese-filled pastry); *yalangi* ("ya-LAWN-gee," grape leaves stuffed with seasoned rice); various dips made from beans, seeds, yogurt, eggplant, and hot peppers; flatbread to eat the dips with; and various kinds of salads, including tabouleh, a Middle Eastern specialty. The menu is the same for breakfast, lunch, and dinner, except for a few things, such as *fool* (fava beans cooked in oil, lemon juice, and garlic, then topped with yogurt) and *fatteh* ("FAT-teh," a slightly sour concoction similar to hot breakfast cereal), that are eaten for breakfast. Then there is always a tray of pickles, olives, mint, and raw vegetables—usually radishes and green peppers.

Only a few restaurants serve fish, and it is quite expensive; the Mediterranean off the coast of Syria is not rich in seafood and has no shellfish at all.

Only a few restaurants serve alcohol, but soda is immensely popular, and Syrians drink it with all meals—even breakfast! They call it all cola.

SNACKS

There are no western-style fast food franchises in Syria, but there is fast food. All Syrian cities have small shops that make a sort of Syrian burrito called *shawarma* ("SHAH-war-ma"). This is thinly-sliced lamb or chicken with garnishes rolled up in a small piece of flatbread. Another type of shop sells felafel sandwiches—crumbled felafel mixed with yogurt, parsley, and other items and also rolled up in flat bread. Chicken shops sell whole roasted birds stuffed with rice or cracked-wheat mixtures as well as fried chicken.

Starting in early spring, there are decorated carts on streetcorners that sell unripened almonds, a sour treat dipped in salt. After the season for almonds is over, the vendors sell unripened plums that look something like green cherry tomatoes. The cart venders also sell corn on the cob. On hot summer evenings people taking their nightly strolls munch on the corn. A few carts also offer coconuts and roasted chestnuts.

In late summer, streetcorner stands are put up to sell ripe prickly pears, and the stand owner peels them in such a way that a person can eat the delicious fruit without the stickers.

Finally, there are hundreds of juice shops where fresh juice or juice and milk drinks are made and served by the bottle or glass. Banana-milk and strawberry-milk are favorites.

A drinks vendor carries a large container filled with coffee or tea for thirsty passers-by.

119

ARTICHOKES WITH GROUND MEAT

juice of 1 lemon
6 artichokes, fresh or canned
$^1/_2$ pound (.23 kg) ground lamb or beef
1 large onion, chopped
handful of pine nuts
medium white sauce (see below)
1 cup grated cheese (gruyère is best)

Cook artichokes in lightly salted boiling water and the lemon juice for 20 minutes or until tender if fresh, five minutes if canned. Drain, scoop out the insides, and place in a greased baking dish. Lightly brown pine nuts and onion in a small amount of butter; drain and set aside. Fry the meat until brown and add pine nuts and onion. Fill the artichokes with the meat mixture. Top with white sauce and grated cheese. Bake at 350° F until tops are lightly browned.

White sauce:

2 tablespoons butter
2 tablespoons flour
$^1/_4$ teaspoon salt
1 cup milk

Melt butter in saucepan over low heat. Blend in flour, salt, and dash of white pepper. Add milk all at once. Cook quickly, stirring constantly until mixture thickens and bubbles.

TRADITIONALISM IN FOODS

The Syrian people, as a rule, are extremely picky about what they eat, and most of them do not even like to try different kinds of food. An exception to this is that many city dwellers (especially teenagers) like pizza, hamburgers, and hot dogs, although these are noticeably different from those in the United States.

As in most other arts, tradition rules in cooking. An example: yogurt is a large part of the diet, used in several different types of dips, as a topping on various dishes, and as a drink mixed with water, salt, and garlic; Syrians even eat plain yogurt by itself. Yet the idea of mixing it with fruit in a blender to make a drink, eating it with fruit or jam mixed in, or using it on a baked potato sounds disgusting to most Syrians. It should only be eaten the way they have traditionally eaten it.

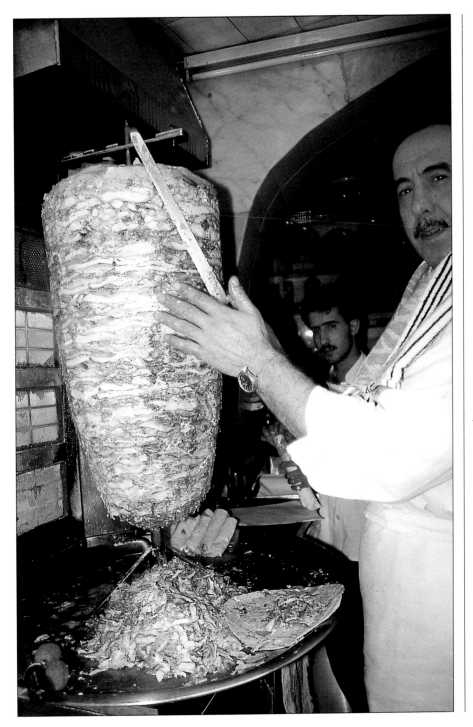

Have you heard the story of Abraham's honored guests? They went in to him and said, "Peace!" "Peace!" he answered and, seeing that they were strangers, betook himself to his family and returned with a fatted calf. He set it before them, saying, "Will you not eat?"

—*The Koran*

Cutting strips of meat in the souk

SYRIA

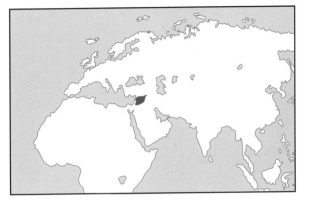

QUICK NOTES

OFFICIAL NAME
The Syrian Arab Republic

AREA
71,500 square miles (185,900 sq km)

POPULATION
13,000,000 million (1993)

CAPITAL
Damascus

NATIONAL SYMBOL
The falcon

NATIONAL FLAG
A white stripe between a red and a black stripe, with two green stars near the center

MAIN CITIES
Damascus, Aleppo, Homs, Latakia, Hama, Al-Kamishli, Rakka, Deir-ez-Zor, Tartous

MAJOR RIVERS
The Euphrates, Al-Khabur, Al-Balikh, the Orontes, the Barada

MAJOR LAKES
Al Asad, Qattina, Al Rastan, Baloran, Arram, Mzerib, Karma, Karn

MAJOR OASIS
Tadmor

HIGHEST POINT
Mt. Hermon, 9,232 feet (2,814 m)

MAJOR RELIGION
Islam (Sunni)

NATIONAL LANGUAGE
Arabic

OFFICIAL LANGUAGE
Arabic

CURRENCY
Syrian lira (or pound); $1=42 lira.

RULING PARTY
Ba'th Party

MAJOR LEADER
Hafez Al Asad, president since 1971

MAIN EXPORTS
Oil, cotton, textiles

IMPORTANT ANNIVERSARIES
Revolution Day, March 8
Birth of the Arab League, March 22
Martyrs Day, April 6
Evacuation Day, April 17
National Day of Mourning, November 29

IMPORTANT RELIGIOUS HOLIDAYS
Easter (variable)
Eid al-Fitr (variable)
Eid al-Adha (variable)
Muharram (variable)
Christmas (December 25)

GLOSSARY

Abu
A title meaning "father of," taken by a man after the birth of a son.

baksbesh ("buk-SHEESH")
A bribe or tip.

Bilad al Sham ("bi-LAD ush-SHAM")
Arabic name for Syria.

Eid al-Adha ("ah-EED al AD-thah")
Muslim festival at the end of hajj, celebrating Abraham's near-sacrifice of Isaac.

Eid al-Fitr ("ah-EED al FIT-ur")
Muslim festival at the end of Ramadan, celebrating the breaking of the fast.

hajj ("haaj")
Pilgrimage to Mecca, one of the five pillars of Islam.

iftar
The evening meal that breaks the daily fast during Ramadan.

insha'Allah ("in-SHAH-al-LAH")
A common Arabic expression, meaning "God willing."

kafeeyeh ("ku-FEE-yea")
A wrapped cotton headdress frequently worn by Syrian men.

Muharram ("moo-ha-RAM")
The Muslim New Year, celebrating the departure of Mohammad for Mecca.

Ramadan ("RAH-mah-dan")
The ninth month of the Islamic calendar, during which Muslims fast from sunrise to sunset.

salat ("sa-LAAT")
Prayer five times daily, one of the five pillars of Islam.

sawm ("soom")
Fasting during Ramadan, one of the five pillars of Islam.

shahada ("sha-HAA-da")
The declaration that there is only one God and that Mohammad was his last prophet, one of the five pillars of Islam.

sharia ("shah-ree-AH")
The Muslim code, a legal system based on the prescriptions of the Koran.

Shi'a ("SHEE-ah")
A Muslim sect believing in the divine right of the caliphs.

souk ("sook")
A traditional marketplace.

Sunni ("SOON-ee")
A Muslim sect believing in election of the caliphs.

zakat ("za-CAT")
An annual tithe of 2.5% of earnings above basic necessities, one of the five pillars of Islam.

BIBLIOGRAPHY

Ball, Barbara, M. Brawer, A. Kartin, S. Postavsky, and Z. Stossel, eds. *Atlas of the Middle East.* New York: MacMillan, 1988.

Gumley, Frances. *The Pillars of Islam: An Introduction to the Islamic Faith.* London: BBC Books, 1990.

Lerner Publications. *Syria—In pictures.* Minneapolis: Lerner Publications, 1990.

Pipes, Daniel. *Greater Syria: The History of an Ambition.* New York: Oxford University Press, 1990.

Raintree Publishers. *Civilizations of the Middle East.* Milwaukee: Raintree Publishers, 1989.

INDEX

INDEX

INDEX